W9-BZV-424

Short Bike Rides™
in Rhode Island

Praise for previous editions:

"Awaken the adventure in yourself by using *Short Bike Rides in Rhode Island* to plan out a bicycle route that will let you truly discover Rhode Island. . . . Stone's delightful dialogue makes this an easy reader. Stone's thorough descriptions include historical glimpses of the state."

—*Rhode Island Herald*

"Each [of his bike books] involves hours of research using topographic maps and countless hours of road-testing each ride mainly for safety and pleasantness."

—*Sunday Journal* (RI) *Magazine*

"Wonderfully illustrated with black-and-white photographs and sample routes."

—*Library Journal*

"If you're a bicyclist and want to fully enjoy the colorful change of the seasons, I strongly recommend taking a copy of *Short Bike Rides in Rhode Island* with you."

—*Rhode Island Woman* magazine

"Keeps you organized and informed as you pedal through the back roads."

—*Women's Sports and Fitness* magazine

Help Us Keep This Guide Up to Date

Every effort has been made by the author and editors to make this guide as accurate and useful as possible. However, many things can change after a guide is published—establishments close, phone numbers change, facilities come under new management, and so on.

We would love to hear from you concerning your experiences with this guide and how you feel it could be made better and be kept up to date. While we may not be able to respond to all comments and suggestions, we'll take them to heart, and we'll also make certain to share them with the author. Please send your comments and suggestions to the following address:

The Globe Pequot Press
Reader Response/Editorial Department
P.O. Box 480
Guilford, CT 06437

Or you may e-mail us at:

editorial@GlobePequot.com

Thanks for your input, and happy travels!

Short Bike Rides® Series

Short Bike Rides™ in Rhode Island

Sixth Edition

Howard Stone

The Globe Pequot Press

GUILFORD, CONNECTICUT

Cover design Saralyn D'Amato-Twomey
Cover photo Chris Dubé

Library of Congress Cataloging-in-Publication Data
Stone, Howard.
    Short bike rides in Rhode Island / by Howard Stone.—6th ed.
        p.   cm. (Short bike rides series)
    ISBN 978-0-7627-0334-0
    1. Bicycle touring—Rhode Island—Guidebooks. 2. Rhode Island—
    Guidebooks. I. Title II. Series.
    GV1045.5.R4S8   1998
    917.4504'43—DC21   98-45531
                                                                    CIP

Manufactured in the United States of America
Sixth Edition/Fourth Printing

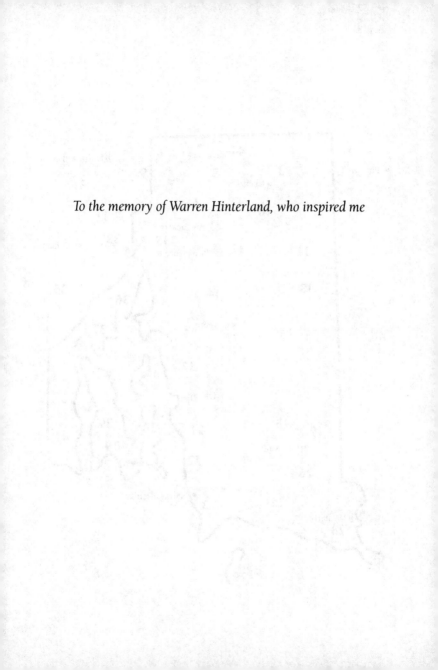

To the memory of Warren Hinterland, who inspired me

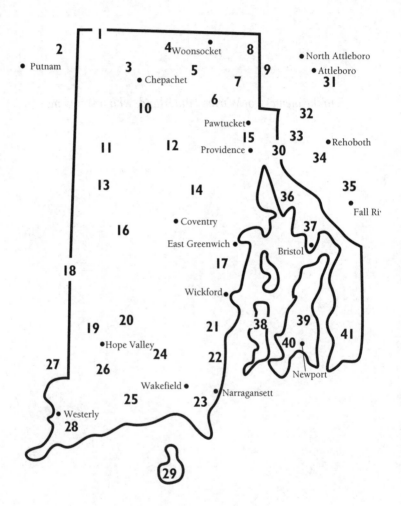

2 Putnam

1

4 Woonsocket

8

3

5

7

9

North Attleboro

Attleboro

31

Chepachet

6

10

32

Pawtucket

15

33

Rehoboth

11

12

Providence

30

34

35

13

14

36

Fall Ri

Coventry

37

16

East Greenwich

Bristol

18

17

Wickford

20

21

38

39

41

19

Hope Valley

24

22

40

Newport

27

26

Wakefield

25

23

Narragansett

28

Westerly

29

Contents

Preface to the Sixth Edition

The sixth edition of *Short Bike Rides in Rhode Island* follows the same format as the earlier editions, with an introductory description, map, and point-to-point directions for each ride. The rides are essentially the same, but the maps and directions have been updated for accuracy and clarity. I have changed the route slightly in some of the rides to take advantage of better roads or to improve safety and scenery.

In response to the suggestion of several riders, I have reinstituted two rides from previous editions: the spectacular Putnam–Woodstock–Thompson ride in Connecticut, and the relaxing Seekonk–Attleboro–Mansfield–Norton ride.

I would like to thank Dominique Coulombe, my supervisor, for allowing me to work flexible hours so that I could take advantage of the daylight to go over the rides. I would also like to thank my wife, Bernice, for her continuous patience, encouragement, and support.

Acknowledgments

Many of the rides were originally mapped out in whole or in part by the following members of the Narragansett Bay Wheelmen, to whom I extend my thanks:

Ted Ellis—Rides 1, 2, 19

John Lanik—Ride 4

Tom Bowater—Rides 5, 11, 21, 25

Earl St. Pierre—Ride 9

Ray Young—Ride 10

Warren Hinterland—Rides 14, 26

Tom Boyden—Ride 16

Ken Becket—Ride 17

Phil Maker—Rides 23, 31

Jack McCue—Rides 30, 36

Ed Ames—Rides 34, 41

Bob Vasconcellos—Ride 37

Bob Corwin—Ride 40

Many of the improvements and modifications to the rides in the earlier editions were suggested by Jack Fahey. Leesa Mann and my wife, Bernice, helped me verify many of the rides for accuracy.

Introduction

Bicycling is an ideal way to appreciate the New England landscape's unique intimacy, which is not found in most other parts of the United States. The back roads turn constantly as they hug the minute contours of the land, forcing your orientation down to a small scale. Every turn and dip in the road may yield a surprise—a weathered barn, a pond, a stream, a little dam or falls, a hulking old Victorian mill right out of the Industrial Revolution, a stone wall, or a pasture with grazing cattle or horses. Many of the smaller town centers are architectural gems, with the traditional stately white church and village green flanked by graceful old wooden homes and the town hall.

Rhode Island, along with the sections of Massachusetts and Connecticut adjoining the state line, offers ideal cycling. The area is blessed with an impressive network of hundreds of back roads, most of them paved but not heavily traveled. Beyond the Providence metropolitan area the landscape is rural enough to give the cyclist a sense of remoteness and serenity, and yet the nearest town, village, or grocery store is never more than a few miles away. The terrain is refreshingly varied for such a small area.

The eastern border of Rhode Island, and nearby Massachusetts, contains flat and gently rolling farmland, with some large areas of cleared land. The western and northern sections of the state consist primarily of wooded, hilly ridge-and-valley country dotted with ponds, small farms, and mill villages. To the south are some of the finest beaches on the East Coast and the beautiful, largely unspoiled shoreline of Narragansett Bay.

The Geography of the Region

Rhode Island is shaped roughly like a triangle with the top chopped off, measuring about 20 miles along the northern border, 35 miles along the southern shore, and 45 miles from north to south along the Connecticut border. Narragansett Bay, Rhode Island's most prominent and scenic natural feature, extends two-thirds of the way up into the state and splits it into two unequal sections, with the segment east of the bay a slender filament only 2 to 5 miles wide. The bay itself contains three large islands and several small ones.

In general, the land east of Narragansett Bay extending into Massachusetts is flat, and everything else is rolling or hilly except for a narrow coastal strip. As a result, biking in Rhode Island involves some effort. Most of the rides contain at least one or two hills, sometimes steep or long enough so that you'll want to walk them. To compensate, however, there are no hills that are long enough to be really discouraging, and for every uphill climb there's a corresponding descent. The majority of the hills you'll encounter are under a half mile long, with the steepest portion being limited to a couple hundred yards or less.

Culturally, Rhode Island is a product of the long and varied history that has nurtured New England. The deep and sheltered waters of Narragansett Bay, which spawned thriving seaports and maritime commerce in colonial times, is now one of the boating capitals of America. The splendid coastline prompted the growth of gracious beachfront communities for the affluent, such as Watch Hill, Narragansett Pier, and the most famous of all, Newport. The Industrial Revolution began in America in 1793 with the Slater Mill in Pawtucket. In later years, culminating in the period between the end of the Civil War and the turn of the century, hundreds more mills were built along the swift-flowing Blackstone, Pawtuxet, Pawcatuck, and other rivers, employing thousands of immigrants from Europe and French Canada.

Today Rhode Island's many mill villages comprise one of the state's most appealing and architecturally fascinating hallmarks. Typically, a mill village contains one or two grim redbrick or granite mills, forbidding but ornamented with cornices and clock towers, and flanked by an orderly row of identical two- and three-story houses, originally built for the workers during the late 1800s. Adjacent to the mill is a small pond with a little dam or falls. Unfortunately, fire, neglect, and vandalism claim several mills each year, but a growing consciousness has arisen toward preserving and maintaining these unique and impressive buildings. Many old mills have been recycled into apartments, condominiums, or offices.

In general, the attitude of the state government and most local communities is favorable toward cyclists. The state's most noteworthy accomplishment is the glorious East Bay Bicycle Path between the Washington Bridge (I–195) in East Providence and Independence Park in Bristol, completed in 1992. The path is well designed and constructed, heavily used, and a delight to ride when not crowded. A more ambitious project, now in the early construction stage, is a 19-mile bikeway along the Blackstone River from the Washington Bridge to Blackstone, Massachusetts. The bikeway, which will run partly on bicycle paths and partly on existing roads, is to be a portion of a linear historical park along the river that will link into a similar project in Massachusetts and ultimately extend to Worcester. Another bikeway under construction will follow a former railroad (called the Washington Secondary) from the Providence–Cranston line southwest through Cranston and West Warwick into Coventry. In southern Rhode Island, the former Narragansett Pier Railroad is being converted into a bikeway between the Kingston train station and Peace Dale, a distance of about 5 miles. Finally, many state and local roads have been resurfaced, and some have been widened with good shoulders.

About the Rides

Ideally, a bicycle ride should be a safe, scenic, relaxing, and enjoyable experience that brings you into intimate contact with the landscape. In striving to achieve this goal, I've routed the rides along paved secondary and rural roads, avoiding main highways, cities, and dirt roads as much as possible. I've tried to make the routes as safe as possible. Hazardous situations such as very bumpy roads or dead stops encountered while riding down a steep hill have been avoided except for a few instances with no reasonable alternate route. Any dangerous spot has been clearly indicated in the directions by a *Caution*. I've included scenic spots like dams, falls, ponds, mill villages, ocean views, or open vistas on the rides wherever possible.

Nearly all the rides have two options—a shorter one averaging about 15 miles and a longer one that is usually between 25 and 30 miles. All the longer rides are extensions of the shorter ones, with both options starting in the same way. A few rides have no shorter option. All the rides make a loop or figure eight rather than going out and then backtracking along the same route. For each ride I include a map and directions.

If you've never ridden any distance, the thought of riding 15, or, heaven forbid, 30 miles may sound intimidating or even impossible. I want to emphasize, however, that *anyone* in normal health can ride 30 miles and enjoy it if you get into a bit of shape first, which you can accomplish painlessly by riding at a leisurely pace for an hour several times a week for two or three weeks. At a moderate pace, you'll ride about 10 miles per hour. If you think of the rides by the hour rather than the mile, the numbers are much less frightening.

To emphasize how easy bicycle riding is, most bike clubs have a 100-mile ride, called a Century, each fall. Dozens of ordinary people try their first Century without ever having done much biking, and finish it, and enjoy it! Sure they're tired at the end, but they've accomplished the feat and loved it. (If you'd like to try one, the Narragansett Bay Wheelmen host the biggest and flattest Century in the Northeast on the Sunday after Labor Day, starting from Tiverton—ask at any bike shop or contact the Narragansett Bay Wheelmen, Box 41177, Providence, RI 02940 for details.)

Not counting long stops, a 15-mile ride should take about two hours at a leisurely speed, a 20- to 25-mile ride about three hours, and a 30-mile ride about four hours. If you ride at a brisk pace, subtract an hour from these estimates.

I have intentionally not listed the hours and fees of historic sites because they are subject to so much change, often from one year to the next. If it's a place you've heard of, it's probably open from 10:00 A.M. to 5:00 P.M., seven days a week. Unfortunately, many of the less frequently visited spots have limited hours—often only weekday afternoons during the summer, and perhaps one day during the weekend. A few places of historic or architectural interest, like the Eleazar Arnold House in Lincoln, are open only by appointment or once a month because of funding and staffing considerations. Most historic sites are maintained only by voluntary contributions and effort, and it's simply impossible to keep them staffed more than a few hours a day or a few months a year. If you really want to visit a site, call beforehand to find out the hours.

About the Maps

The maps are reasonably accurate, but I have not attempted to draw them strictly to scale. Congested areas may be enlarged in relation to the rest of the map for the sake of legibility. All the maps adhere to these conventions:

1. The maps are oriented with North at the top.
2. Route numbers are circled.
3. Small arrows alongside the route indicate direction of travel.
4. The longer ride is marked by a heavy line. The shorter ride is marked by a dotted line where the route differs from that of the longer ride.
5. I've tried to show the angle of forks and intersections as accurately as possible.

Enjoying the Rides

You will enjoy biking more if you add a few basic accessories to your bike and bring a few items with you.

1. **Handlebar bag with transparent map pocket on top**. It's always helpful to have some carrying capacity on your bike. Most handlebar bags are large enough to hold tools, a lunch, or even a light jacket. If you have a map or directions in your map pocket (or taped to the top of the bag), it's much easier to follow the route. You simply glance down instead of fishing a map or directions out of your pocket and stopping to read them safely. You may also wish to get a small saddlebag that fits under your seat, or a metal rack that fits above the rear wheel, to carry whatever doesn't fit in the handlebar bag.

Always carry things on your bike, not on your back. A knapsack raises your center of gravity and makes you more unstable; it also digs painfully into your shoulders if you have more than a couple of pounds in it. It may do for a quick trip to the grocery store or campus, but never for an enjoyable ride where you'll be on the bike for more than a few minutes.

2. Water bottle and/or hydration pack. It is vital to carry water with you—if you don't drink enough water you will dehydrate. Bring two or three water bottles and keep them filled. Put only water in your water bottles—it quenches thirst better than any other liquid.

An excellent alternative or addition to water bottles is a hydration pack worn like a backpack. You drink through a tube conveniently positioned in front of you, eliminating the need to reach down to remove the bottle from your bike. Most hydration packs have the capacity of two or three bottles. It is important to allow the inner reservoir to dry when not in use to prevent mold and mildew; you can buy a flexible frame that will hold it open for this purpose.

3. Basic tools. Always carry a few basic tools with you when you go out for a ride, just in case you get a flat or a loose derailleur cable. Tire irons, a six-inch adjustable wrench, a small pair of pliers, a small standard screwdriver, and a small Phillips-head screwdriver are all you need to take care of virtually all roadside emergencies. A rag and a tube of hand cleaner are useful if you have to touch your chain. If your bike has any Allen nuts (nuts with a small hexagonal socket on top), carry metric Allen wrenches to fit them. Most bicycle shops sells a handy one-piece kit with several Allen wrenches, along with a standard and Phillips-head screwdriver.

4. Pump and spare tube. If you get a flat, you're immobilized unless you can pump up a new tube or patch the old one. Installing a brand new tube is less painful than trying to patch the old one on the road. Do the patching at home. Pump up the tire until it's hard, and you are on your way. Carry the spare tube in your handlebar bag or wind it around the seat post, but make sure it doesn't rub against the rear tire.

If you bike a lot and don't use a mountain bike, you'll get flats—it's a fact of life. Most flats are on the rear wheel, because that's where most of your weight is. You should therefore practice taking the rear wheel off and putting it back on the bike, and taking the tire off and putting it on the rim, until you can do it confidently. It's much easier to practice at home than to fumble at it by the roadside.

5. Dog repellent. When you ride in rural areas you're going to encounter dogs, no two ways about it. Even if you don't have to use it, you'll have peace of mind knowing you have something like ammonia or commercial dog spray to repel an attacking dog if you have to. More on this later.

6. Bicycle computer. A bicycle computer provides a much more reliable way of following a route than depending on street signs or landmarks. Street signs are often nonexistent in rural areas or are rotated 90 degrees by mischievous kids. Landmarks such as "turn right at green house" or "turn left at Ted's Market" lose effectiveness when the green house is repainted red or Ted's Market goes out of business. Most computers indicate not only distance, but also speed, elapsed time, and cadence (revolutions per minute of the pedals). The solar-powered models last a long time before the batteries need replacement.

7. Bike lock. This is a necessity if you're going to leave your bike unattended. The best locks are the rigid, bolt cutter-proof ones like Kryptonite and Citadel. The next best choice is a strong chain or cable that can't be quickly severed by a normal-sized bolt cutter or hacksaw. A cheap, flimsy chain can be cut in a few seconds and is not much better than no lock at all.

In urban or heavily touristed areas, always lock both wheels as well as the frame to a solid object, and take your accessories with you when you leave the bicycle. Many a cyclist ignoring this simple precaution has returned to the vehicle only to find one or both wheels gone, along with the pump, water bottle, and carrying bags.

8. Rearview mirror. A marvelous safety device, available at any bike shop, that enables you to check the situation behind you without turning your head. Once you start using a mirror you'll feel defenseless without it. Most mirrors are designed to fit on either a bike helmet or the handlebars.

9. Bike helmet. Accidents happen, and a helmet will protect your head if you fall or crash. Bike helmets are light and comfortable, and most cyclists use them.

10. Food. Always bring some food with you when you go for a ride. It's surprising how quickly you get hungry when biking. Some of the rides go through remote areas with no food along the way, and that country store you were counting on may be closed on weekends or out of business. Fruit is nourishing and includes a lot of water. A couple of candy bars or pieces of pastry will provide a burst of energy for the last 10 miles if you are getting tired. (Don't eat candy or sweets before then—the energy burst lasts only about an hour, then your blood-sugar level drops to below where it was before and you'll be really weak.)

11. Bicycling gloves. Gloves designed for biking, with padded palms and no fingers, will cushion your hands and protect them if you fall. For maximum comfort, use foam-rubber handlebar padding also.

12. Kickstand. A kickstand makes it easy to stand your bike upright without leaning it against a wall or other object. Keep in mind that a strong wind may knock your bike over and that in hot weather a kickstand may sink far enough into asphalt to topple your bike.

13. Bike rack. It is much easier to use a bike rack than to wrestle your bike into and out of your car or trunk. Racks that attach to the back of the car are most convenient—do you really want to hoist your bike over your head onto the roof? If you use a rack that fits onto the back of your car, make sure that the bike is at least a foot off the ground and that the bicycle tire is well above the tailpipe. Hot exhaust blows out tires!

14. Light. Bring a bicycle light and reflective legbands with you in case you are caught in the dark. Ankle lights are lightweight and bob up and down as you pedal for additional visibility.

15. Fanny pack. Since many cycling shorts and jerseys don't have pockets, a small fanny pack is useful for carrying your keys, a wallet, and loose change.

16. Toilet paper. A must have—for obvious reasons.

17. Roll of electrical tape. You never know when you'll need it.

18. Rhode Island state highway map. This map is useful because it shows every back road and describes points of interest and historic sites. It is available from the Rhode Island Economic Development Corporation, One West Exchange Street, Providence, RI 02903. Free.

If you are not concerned with riding fast, the most practical bicycle for recreational riding is a mountain bike or a hybrid between a mountain bike and a sport bike. Most people find the upright riding position comfortable. The gearing is almost always lower than it is on sport bikes, which makes climbing hills much easier. (If you buy a mountain bike, be sure to get one with eighteen or more speeds.) The shift levers are mounted on the handlebars, so you don't have to move your hands when shifting gears. The fatter, thicker tires are very resistant to punctures and unlikely to get caught in storm-sewer grates. Mountain bikes are more stable, rugged, and resistant to damage than sport bikes. The only disadvantage of mountain bikes is that they are a little slower than other bicycles because of the wider tires and less streamlined riding position.

If most of your riding is done on pavement, you don't need standard mountain bike tires, which are about 2 inches wide with a deep, knobby tread. Use narrower tires (often called city tires or cross-training tires), which are 1⅜ or 1½ inches wide with a fairly smooth tread.

Before you begin riding, adjust your seat to the proper height and make sure it is level. Many riders have the seat too low, which robs you of power and leverage when pedaling and puts harmful strain on your knees. It's best to adjust the seat with a friend who can hold the bike firmly while you mount it in riding position with the pedal arms vertical. When your seat is at the proper height, the knee of your extended leg should be slightly bent when you place the balls of both feet directly over the pedal spindles (the proper placement while riding). Then put both heels on the pedals. Your extended leg should now be straight, and you should be able to backpedal without rocking. If you rock from side to side, the seat is too high; if your leg is still bent with the pedal arms at six and twelve o'clock, the seat is too low.

It's easiest to check whether your seat is level by placing a long board or broom handle on top of it lengthwise. Also check that the seat is not too far forward or back. When the pedal arms are horizontal, your forward knee should be directly over the pedal spindle. Again, a friend is helpful when you make the adjustments.

Take advantage of your gearing when you ride. It's surprising how many people with multispeed bikes use only two or three of their gears. It takes less effort to spin your legs quickly in the low or middle gears than to grind along in your higher ones. For leisurely biking, a rate of about eighty revolutions per minute is comfortable. If you find yourself grinding along at fewer than 75 RPMs, shift into a lower gear. Time your RPMs periodically on a watch with a second hand or your bicycle computer—keeping your cadence up is the best habit you can acquire for efficient cycling. You'll be less tired at the end of a ride and avoid strain on your knees if you use the right gears.

If you have a ten- or twelve-speed bike, you will find it much easier to climb hills if you get a freewheel (the rear cluster of gears) that goes up to thirty-four teeth instead of the standard twenty-eight teeth. You may also have to buy a new rear derailleur to accommodate the larger shifts, but the expense will be more than worthwhile in ease of pedaling. For the ultimate in hill-climbing ease you need a bicycle with eighteen or more speeds. The smaller the inner front chainwheel, the lower the low gear. I recommend a small chainwheel with twenty-four or twenty-six teeth.

When approaching a hill, always shift into low gear *before* the hill, not after you start climbing it. If it's a steep or long hill, get into your lowest gear right away and go slowly to reduce the effort. Don't be afraid to walk up a really tough hill; it's not a contest, and you're out to enjoy yourself.

Pedal with the balls of your feet over the spindles, not your arches or heels. Toe clips are ideal for keeping your feet in the proper position on the pedals; they also give you added leverage when going uphill. Your leg should be slightly bent at the bottom of the downstroke. The straps should be *loose* (or the spring tension on clipless pedals should be low) so that you can take your feet off the pedals effortlessly.

Eat before you get hungry, drink before you get thirsty, and rest before you get tired. A good rule of thumb is to drink one water bottle per hour. To keep your pants out of the chain, tuck them inside your socks. Wear pants that are as seamless as possible. Jeans or cut-offs are the worst offenders; their thick seams are uncomfortable. For maximum comfort wear padded cycling shorts, with no underwear, and cycling tights that fit over the shorts when the temperature is below 60 or 65 degrees. Use a firm, good-quality seat. A soft, mushy seat may feel inviting, but as soon as you sit on it the padding compresses to zero under your weight, so that you're really sitting on a harsh metal shell.

If you have to use the bathroom, the simplest solution is to get out of sight off the road. A footpath or one-lane dirt road that curves out of sight into the woods is ideal. Most fast-food restaurants have easily accessible rest rooms. If a restaurant is of the "Please wait to be seated" variety or has facilities "for customers only," either walk in briskly or order a snack. Most gas stations have rest rooms; most convenience stores and country stores do not, but they will sometimes accommodate you if you ask urgently.

Using the Maps and Directions

Unfortunately, a book format does not lend itself to quick and easy consultation while you're on your bike. The rides will go more smoothly if you don't have to dismount at each intersection to consult the map or directions. You can solve this problem by making a photocopy of the directions and carrying them in your map pocket or taping them on top of your handlebar bag, dismounting occasionally to turn a sheet over or to switch sheets. Most people find it easier to follow the directions than the map.

In the directions, I have indicated the name of a road if there was a visible street sign at the time I researched the route, and I designated the road as "unmarked" if the street sign was absent or not clearly visible (many street signs are visible only from one direction, or are obscured by tree branches or utility poles). Street signs have a short life span—a couple of years on average—and are often nonexistent in rural areas. Any sign with a double entendre, such as cherry, will be adorning some teenager's room within a week. Very frequently, the name of a road changes without warning at a town line, crossroads, or other intersection.

Using a bicycle computer is virtually essential to enjoy the rides. The directions indicate the distance to the next turn or major intersection. Because so many of the roads are unmarked, you'll have to keep track accurately of the distance from one turn to the next. It is helpful to keep in mind that a tenth of a mile is 176 yards, or nearly twice the length of a football field.

In written directions, it is obviously not practical to mention every single intersection. I have not mentioned most crossroads if the route goes straight, nor have I mentioned forks where one branch is clearly the main road. Always stay on the main road unless directed otherwise.

In the directions, certain words occur frequently, so let me define them to avoid any confusion.

To "bear" means to turn diagonally, somewhere between a forty-five-degree angle and going straight ahead. In these illustrations, you bear from road A onto road B.

To "merge" means to come into a road diagonally, or even head-on, if a side road comes into a main road. In the examples, road A merges into road B.

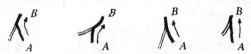

A "sharp" turn is any turn more than ninety degrees; in other words, a hairpin turn or something approaching it. In the examples, it is a sharp turn from road A onto road B.

Each ride contains a few introductory paragraphs that mention points of interest along the route or sometimes a short distance off it. Usually I do not mention these places again in the directions them-

selves to keep them concise. If you'd like to keep aware of points of interest while doing the ride, make a note of them first so you won't have to flip back and forth between the directions and the introduction. It is a good idea to read over the entire tour before taking it, in order to familiarize yourself with the terrain, points of interest, and places requiring caution.

Safety

It is an unfortunate fact that thousands of bicycle accidents occur each year, with many fatalities. Almost all cycling accidents, however, are needless and preventable. Most accidents involve children under sixteen and are caused by foolhardy riding and failure to exercise common sense. The chances of having an accident can be reduced virtually to zero by having your bike in good mechanical condition, using two pieces of safety equipment (a rearview mirror and a helmet), being aware of the most common biking hazards, and not riding at night unless prepared for it.

Before going out for a ride, be sure your bike is mechanically sound. Its condition is especially important if you bought the bike at a discount store, where it was probably assembled by a high school kid with no training. Above all, be sure that the wheels are secure and the brakes work. If your wheels are fastened with quick-release levers, be certain that they are clamped properly. If you're not sure how to do this, ask someone at a bike shop to show you; your safety depends on it.

Be certain that your shoelaces are firmly tied, or use footwear with Velcro closures. A loose shoelace can wrap around the pedal axle or get caught in the chain, trapping you on the bicycle.

Invest in a rearview mirror and a bicycle helmet, both available at any bike shop. Most mirrors attach to either your helmet or your handlebars and work as well as car mirrors when properly adjusted. The greatest benefit of having a mirror is that when you come to an obstacle, such as a pothole or a patch of broken glass, you can tell at a glance whether or not it's safe to swing out into the road to avoid it. On narrow or winding roads you can always be aware of the traffic behind you and plan accordingly. Best of all, a mirror eliminates the need to peek back over your shoulder—an action that is potentially dangerous because you sometimes unconsciously veer toward the middle of the road while peeking. Helmets are legally required for children in Rhode Island, Massachusetts, and Connecticut.

A bicycle helmet is the cyclist's cheapest form of life insurance. A helmet not only protects your head if you land on it after a fall, but also protects against the sun and the rain. All responsible cyclists wear them, and so you shouldn't feel afraid of looking odd if you use one. Helmets are light and comfortable; once you get used to one, you'll never even know you have it on.

While on the road, use the same plain old common sense that you use while driving a car. Stop signs and traffic lights are there for a reason—obey them. At intersections, give cars the benefit of the doubt rather than trying to dash out in front of them or beat them through the light. Remember, they're bigger, heavier, and faster than you are. And you're out to enjoy yourself and get some exercise, not to be king of the road.

Several situations are inconsequential to the motorist, but potentially hazardous for the bicyclist. When biking, try to keep aware of these:

1. **Road surface.** Most roads in Rhode Island are not silk-smooth. Often the bicyclist must contend with bumps, ruts, cracks, potholes, and fish-scale sections of road that have been patched and repatched numerous times. When the road becomes rough, the only prudent course of action is to slow down and keep alert, especially going downhill. Riding into a deep pothole or wheel-swallowing crack can cause a nasty spill. On bumps, you can relieve some of the shock by getting up off the seat.

2. **Sand patches.** Patches of sand often build up at intersections, sharp curves, the bottom of hills, and sudden dips in the road. Sand

is very unstable if you're turning, so slow way down, stop pedaling, and keep in a straight line until you're beyond the sandy spot.

3. Storm-sewer grates. Federal regulations have outlawed thousands of hazardous substances and products, but unfortunately they have not yet outlawed the storm-sewer grates parallel to the roadway. This is a very serious hazard, because a cyclist catching the wheel in a slot will instantly fall, probably in a somersault over the handlebars. Storm sewers are relatively rare in rural areas, but always a very real hazard.

4. Dogs. Unfortunately, man's best friend is the cyclist's worst enemy. When riding in the country you will encounter dogs, pure and simple. Even though many communities have leash laws, they are usually not enforced unless a dog seriously injures someone or annoys its owners' neighbors enough that they complain—a rare situation because the neighbors probably all have dogs, too.

The best defense against a vicious dog is to carry repellent—either ammonia in a squirtgun or plant sprayer (make sure it is leakproof), or a commercial dog spray called Halt, an extract of hot peppers that comes in an aerosol can and is available at most bike shops. Repellent is effective only if you can grab it instantly when you need it—*don't* put it in your handlebar pack, a deep pocket, or anyplace else where you'll have to fish around for it. For Halt to work you have to squirt it directly into the dog's eyes, but if the dog is close enough to really threaten you it's easily done.

The main danger from dogs is not being bitten, but rather bumping into them or instinctively veering toward the center of the road into oncoming traffic when the dog comes after you. Fortunately, almost all dogs have a sense of territory and will not chase you more than a tenth of a mile. If you're going along at a brisk pace in front of the dog when it starts to chase you, you can probably outrun it and stay ahead until you reach the animal's territorial limit. If you are going at a leisurely pace, however, or heading uphill, or the dog is in the road in front of you, the only safe thing to do is dismount and walk slowly forward, keeping the bike between you and the dog, until you leave its territory. If the dog is truly menacing, or there's more than one, repellent can be comforting to have.

If you decide to stay on the bike when a dog chases you, always get into low gear and spin your legs as quickly as possible. It's hard for a dog to bite a fast-rotating target. Many cyclists swing their pump at the animal, but this increases the danger of losing control of your bike. Often, yelling "Stay!" or "No!" in an authoritative voice will make a dog back off.

5. Undivided, shoulderless, four-lane highways. This is the most dangerous type of road for biking. If traffic is very light there is no problem, but in moderate or heavy traffic the road becomes a death trap unless you ride assertively. The only safe way to travel on such a road is to stay in or near the center of the right lane, rather than at the edge, forcing traffic coming up behind you to pass you in the lane to your left. If you hug the right-hand edge, some motorists will not get out of the right lane, brushing past you by inches or even forcing you off the road. Some drivers mentally register a bicycle as being only as wide as its tire, an unsettling image when the lane is not much wider than a car.

Several rides in this book contain short stretches along highways. If traffic is heavy enough to occupy both lanes most of the time, the only truly safe thing to do is walk your bike along the side of the road.

6. Railroad tracks. Tracks that cross the road at an oblique angle are a severe hazard, because you can easily catch your wheel in the slot between the rails and fall. *Never* ride diagonally across tracks—either walk your bike across, or, if no traffic is in sight, cross the tracks at right angles by swerving into the road. When riding across tracks, slow down and get up off the seat to relieve the shock of the bump.

7. Oiled and sanded roads. Many communities occasionally spread a film of oil or tar over the roads to seal cracks and then spread sand over the road to absorb the oil. The combination is treacherous for biking. Be very careful, especially going downhill. If the sand is deep or if the tar or oil is still sticky, you should walk.

8. Car doors opening into your path. This is a severe hazard in urban areas and in the center of towns. To be safe, any time you ride past a line of parked cars, stay 4 or 5 feet away from them. If oncoming traffic won't permit this, proceed very slowly and notice whether the driver's seat of each car is occupied. A car pulling to the side of the road in front of you is an obvious candidate for trouble.

9. Low sun. If you're riding directly into a low sun, traffic behind you may not see you, especially through a smeared or dirty windshield. Here your rearview mirror becomes a lifesaver, because the only safe way to proceed is to glance constantly in the mirror and remain aware of conditions behind you. If you are riding directly away from a low sun, traffic coming toward you may not see you and could make a left turn into your path. If the sun is on your right or left, drivers on your side may not see you, and a car could pull out from a side road into your path. To be safe, give any traffic that may be blinded by the sun the benefit of the doubt, and dismount if necessary. Because most of the roads you'll be on are winding and wooded, you won't run into blinding sun frequently, but you should remain aware of the problem.

10. Kids on bikes. Children riding on their bikes in circles in the middle of the road and shooting in and out of driveways are a hazard; the risk of collision is always there because they aren't watching where they're going. Any time you see kids playing in the street, especially if they're on bikes, be prepared for anything and call out "Beep-beep" or "Watch out" as you approach. If you have a loud bell or horn, use it.

11. Wet leaves. In the fall, wet leaves are slippery. Avoid turning on them.

12. Metal-grate bridges. When wet, metal grating becomes slippery, and you may be in danger of falling and injuring yourself. If the road is wet, or early in the morning when there may be condensation on the bridge, please walk across.

A few additional safety reminders: If bicycling in a group, ride single file and at least 20 feet apart. Use hand signals when turning—to signal a right turn, stick out your right arm. If you stop to rest or examine your bike, get both your bicycle and yourself completely off the road. Sleek black bicycle clothing is stylish, but bright colors are more visible and safer.

Finally, use common courtesy toward motorists and pedestrians. Hostility toward bicyclists has received national media attention; it is caused by the 2 percent who are discourteous cyclists (mainly messengers and groups hogging the road), who give the other 98 percent—responsible riders—a bad image. Please do not be part of the 2 percent!

The Narragansett Bay Wheelmen

If you would like to bike with a group and meet other people who enjoy cycling, the Narragansett Bay Wheelmen (NBW), the main bicycle club for the Rhode Island area, welcomes you on any of its rides, which are held on Sunday mornings. The rides include many of the tours in this book and others a little farther into Massachusetts and Connecticut. You ride at your own pace, and there is never any pressure or competition to ride farther or faster than you wish. There is always a short ride of under 20 miles if you don't want to tackle a longer ride. You can't get lost, because for every ride arrows are painted on the road at the turns, and maps are handed out.

Rides are sometimes announced in the listing of weekend sports events in the *Providence Journal* on Fridays or Saturdays. You don't have to be a member to ride with the NBW, but the dues are nominal and by joining you get the club's bimonthly publication, The *Spoke 'n Word*, which lists upcoming rides for a couple months in advance and contains articles and news of the local biking scene. For more information, write to the NBW at P. O. Box 41177, Providence, RI 02940; or visit its Web site at http://www.aljian.com/nbw/

The NBW also has an advocacy committee devoted to improving conditions for bicyclists. Activities include having a voice in the planning of bikeways and road construction projects, replacement of unsafe sewer grates, and bicycle safety education.

Other Organizations

Pequot Cyclists, Box 505, Gales Ferry, CT 06335. Based in southeastern Connecticut, with some rides in southwestern Rhode Island.

League of American Bicyclists, 1612 K Street NW, Suite 401, Washington, DC 20006. The main national organization of and for bicyclists. Excellent monthly magazine, dynamic legislative action program.

Bikeways

There is currently only one bona fide bikeway, or bicycle path, in Rhode Island, although others are being planned and constructed. The East Bay Bicycle Path runs for about 13.5 miles from the East Providence end of the Washington Bridge (I–195) to Independence Park in Bristol. Although this bikeway is well designed and well maintained, *caution* is necessary when riding along it because it is very heavily used by both cyclists and noncyclists. In good weather the path is crowded with riders of all levels of experience, including young children wobbling along or weaving from one side of the path to the other. Inexperienced riders often stop suddenly on the bikeway without warning. The path is also heavily used by pedestrians, joggers, skaters, skateboarders, dogs, and playing children.

When passing, call out "Passing on your left" or "Coming through" in a loud, clear voice. The bikeway crosses some busy roads, so be careful at intersections and dismount if appropriate. Keep your pace moderate. I suggest using the bikeway early in the morning before it becomes busy, or when the weather is less than ideal for cycling.

Feedback

I'd be grateful for any comments, criticisms, or suggestions about the rides in this book. Road conditions change, and a new snack bar or point of interest may open up along one of the routes. An intersection may be changed by road construction or improvement, or a traffic light may be installed. I'd like to keep the book updated by incorporating changes as they occur or modifying a route if necessary in the interest of safety. Many of the changes in each new edition are in response to riders' suggestions. Please feel free to contact me through The Globe Pequot Press, P.O. Box 833, Old Saybrook, Connecticut 06475 with any revision you think helpful.

About the Author

Howard Stone grew up in Boston, went to college in Maine and Illinois, and returned to his native New England, where he is now a librarian at Brown University. For many years Howard was the touring director of the Narragansett Bay Wheelmen, the major bicycle club for Rhode Island and southeastern Massachusetts. He is the author of *Short Bike Rides in Eastern Massachusetts,* and *Short Bike Rides in Western Massachusetts,* also published by The Globe Pequot Press, and two other bicycling guides. Howard has done extensive bicycle touring, including a cross-country trip from Newport, Oregon, to Newport, Rhode Island, in 1978.

Tri-State Tour
Pascoag–Douglas–Webster–Sutton

Number of miles:	18 (33 with tri-state extension)
Terrain:	Rolling, with one tough hill. The long ride has an additional hill.
Start:	Municipal parking lot in Pascoag, next to the post office, 1 block north of junction of Routes 107 and 100.
Food:	None on short ride until end. Friendly's Ice Cream, corner of Routes 12, 193, and 16, Webster. Small grocery at Sutton Falls Campground, Manchaug Road, Sutton, open during camping season. Country store on Holt Road in Sutton.

This is a tour of the mostly wooded and lake-studded countryside surrounding the point where Rhode Island, Connecticut, and Massachusetts meet. The terrain is not as hilly as in the areas to the south and west. The lightly traveled back roads, winding through woods and along several ponds, promise enjoyable and peaceful bicycling.

The ride starts from the attractive little mill town of Pascoag, which is typical of the many mill villages throughout Rhode Island. Leaving Pascoag, pass an old red schoolhouse, and climb gradually to the top of Buck Hill, one of Rhode Island's highest points, with an elevation of 730 feet.

The ride down the western side is a thriller. You'll soon enter the northeastern corner of Connecticut. After about 3 miles of narrow lanes, cross the Massachusetts line into Webster, a small mill city. As you head toward town on Route 193, you'll follow Lake Chargoggagoggmanchaugagoggchaubunagungamaug, which in the Nipmuc Indian language means, "I fish on my side, you fish on your side, and

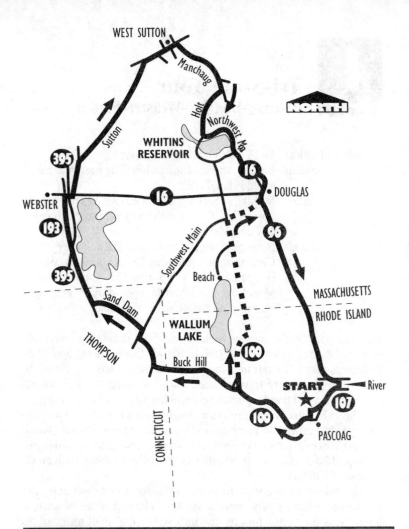

NORTH

WEST SUTTON

Manchaug

Holt

Northwest Ma

WHITINS
RESERVOIR

16

395

16

DOUGLAS

WEBSTER

96

193

Southwest Main

Beach

395

Sand Dam

MASSACHUSETTS

RHODE ISLAND

THOMPSON

WALLUM
LAKE

Buck Hill

100

START ★

River

100

107

CONNECTICUT

PASCOAG

HOW to get there
Take Route 44 to Chepachet. Bear right on Route 102 (from the west, turn sharp left). Just ahead, go straight on Route 100 for 3 miles to Route 107. Turn right and go 0.1 mile to the first legal left. Go 1 block to end. Turn right, and parking lot is immediately ahead on right.

DIREC-TIONS

for the ride

33 miles

- Left out of parking lot for 1 block to end (Route 100 on right).
- Turn right and just ahead right again on main road. Go 3.2 miles to Buck Hill Road, which bears left (sign may say TO CONNECTICUT ROUTE 12). Here the short ride goes straight.
- Bear left for 0.1 mile to fork (main road bears left).
- Bear left for 3 miles to end, at bottom of second long descent.
- Right for 1.2 miles to end, at church.
- Right and just ahead bear left at fork on Sand Dam Road. Go 2 miles to end (Route 193), at stop sign.
- Bear right for 3 miles to third traffic light (Routes 16 and 12). Friendly's Ice Cream on far left corner.
- Right (left if coming from Friendly's) for 0.3 mile to Sutton Road on left, just past I–395 underpass.
- Left for 0.3 mile to where Sutton Road turns right.
- Right for 3.8 miles to end.
- Right for 0.2 mile to fork (main road bears slightly left downhill).
- Bear left for 1 mile to second right (Manchaug Road), which is almost at bottom of long downhill (sign may say SUTTON FALLS CAMP-ING AREA).
- Right for 2.3 miles to fork where Torrey Road goes straight down steep hill.
- Straight for 0.3 mile to Holt Road on right.
- Right for 1.3 miles to fork where Wallis Street bears right and Northwest Main Street bears left.
- Bear left for 0.7 mile to another fork. You'll follow the Whitins Reservoir on your right and pass a water slide after 0.2 mile.
- Bear right, following pond on right, for 0.8 mile to end (merge left on Wallis Street). There is no stop sign here.
- Bear left for 0.6 mile to fork.
- Bear left for 0.4 mile to fork (church on right), in the village center of Douglas.
- Bear right for 0.1 mile to end (merge right onto Route 16). Immedi-

ately ahead Route 16 turns right, but go straight for 50 yards to fork where Route 96 (South Street) bears left.

- Bear left for 6.6 miles to end, at stop sign. Route 96 turns left here.
- Left and just ahead right on River Street for 0.1 mile to end (Route 107, Chapel Street).
- Bear right and stay on main road for 1.4 miles to end, opposite supermarket. Route 107 twists and turns, but stay on main road.
- Turn right. Parking lot is immediately ahead on right.

18 miles

- Follow first 2 directions of long ride.
- Straight on Route 100 for 2.2 miles to stop sign where main road turns 90 degrees left.
- Left for 3.1 miles to crossroads and stop sign (Southwest Main Street). *Caution:* Bumpy Spots. Beach on Wallum Lake if you turn left after 2.2 miles into Douglas State Forest; go 1 mile to beach.
- Right for 1.3 miles to stop sign; Route 96 (South Street) turns sharply right here. Village of Douglas is just ahead if you go straight.
- Sharp right on Route 96 for 6.6 miles to end, at stop sign. Route 96 turns left here.
- Left and just ahead right on River Street for 0.1 mile to end (Route 107, Chapel Street).
- Follow last 2 directions of long ride.

---

nobody fishes in the middle."

Skirting the edge of Webster, quickly head into rolling, wooded countryside to the tiny village of West Sutton. Here you will pass Sutton Falls, a small dam with a little covered bridge above it. Just ahead are pleasant roads along Manchaug Pond and the Whitins Reservoir, where you'll pass a water slide (here's your chance to descend a different type of hill). From here it's not far to the graceful, classic New England village of Douglas, marked by a stately white church, old cemetery, and triangular green. From Douglas follow a lightly trav-

eled secondary road, Route 96, back to Pascoag.

The short ride bypasses Buck Hill and Connecticut by heading north directly into Massachusetts. Just before the state line is Zambarano Hospital, a state institution for the severely retarded and handicapped. You climb sharply into Douglas, where you pick up Route 96 for the return trip to Pascoag. A beach on Wallum Lake, in Douglas State Forest, is a mile off the route.

2 Putnam–Woodstock–Thompson, Connecticut

Number of miles: 16 (34 with Woodstock extension)
          Terrain: Rolling with a tough hill near the end. The 34-mile ride is hilly.
            Start: Pulaski Memorial Recreation Area, off Pulaski Road in West Glocester, at Connecticut line.
             Food: Snack bar at corner of Routes 21 and 44. Snack bar on Route 169, Woodstock (long ride). Restaurant on Route 12 near Route 193. Restaurant in Thompson. Snack bar at crossroads near end of ride.

On this ride, you'll explore the inspiringly beautiful ridge-and-valley country in the northeastern corner of Connecticut just west of the Rhode Island border. The long ride goes through some of the finest scenery in the book. The rolling terrain is somewhat challenging, but the panoramic views from the hilltops and some exhilarating descents will more than reward your efforts. Here is rural New England at its best—rambling old farmhouses, weathered red barns with woodpiles neatly stacked beside them, and stone walls zigzagging across sloping fields filled with grazing cows and horses.

   Pulaski Memorial Recreation Area, a large expanse of woodland on the Connecticut border with a small beach, is a good place to begin the ride. Just after you leave the park you cross into Connecticut, heading west on small hillside lanes with fine views of the neighboring ridges. After several miles, the short ride heads north to the handsome town of Thompson, a traditional New England village

with a white church, a stone library, and the elegant Vernon Stiles Inn (a good food stop) clustered around the green. Two miles out of town off the route is the Thompson Speedway, one of New England's leading automobile racetracks.

Shortly after you leave Thompson, you ascend onto a ridge with a spectacular view and zip down the far side to the Quaddick Reservoir, which straddles both sides of the narrow road. From here, it's two miles up and down a steep wooded hill back to the starting point and a swim in the pond.

The long ride continues into Connecticut, first reaching Putnam, an old mill town with an impressive dam across the Quinebaug River. In the center of town are several antiques shops, a bicycle shop, and an old train station that has been renovated into offices. From Putnam it's several miles to the unspoiled hilltop town of Woodstock, a classic New England jewel. Framing the large green are a stately white church, the handsome main building of Woodstock Academy, and the Bowen House. This ornate, pink Gothic mansion (also called Roseland Cottage) was built in 1846 by Henry C. Bowen, a businessman who entertained several Presidents there at Fourth of July gatherings during the 1880s and 1890s. Before you leave Woodstock, ride 100 yards down a service road alongside one of Woodstock Academy's buildings for a superb view of the area.

You'll exult in the sustained mile-long descent out of Woodstock. At the bottom, turn north on Dugg Hill Road, a lane that climbs up to a ridge with inspiring views of the rolling countryside. A few miles farther on, ride along the top of West Thompson Dam, high above its lake, before climbing out of the valley to Thompson, where you rejoin the short ride.

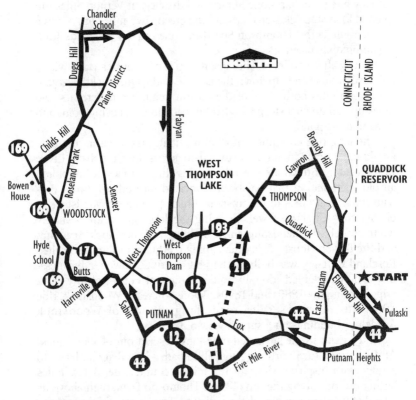

Chandler School

NORTH

Dugg Hill

Paine District

Fabyan

CONNECTICUT

RHODE ISLAND

169

Childs Hill

Roseland Park

Senexet

WEST THOMPSON LAKE

Gawron

Brandy Hill

QUADDICK RESERVOIR

Bowen House

169

WOODSTOCK

West Thompson

THOMPSON

Quaddick

193

Hyde School

171

Butts

West Thompson Dam

21

169

Harrisville

Sabin

171

12

East Putnam

Elmwood Hill

★START

Pulaski

PUTNAM

Fox

44

12

Five Mile River

44

Putnam Heights

44

12

21

HOW to get there
From the east, head west on Route 44 until you come to Route 94 on your left. Continue on Route 44 for another mile to Pulaski Road on your right. Then turn right onto Pulaski Road and go one mile to park. There are three parking lots about a quarter of a mile along the park access road. Park in the third lot, which adjoins a small pond with a beach.

From the west go east on Route 44 to the Rhode Island border, then take your first left onto Pulaski Road.

DIREC-TIONS
for the ride

34 miles

- At end of park entrance road, go straight on Pulaski Road for 0.8 mile to end (Route 44).
- Right for 0.3 mile to Putnam Heights Road, which bears left.
- Bear left and stay on main road for 1.7 miles to crossroads and stop sign (East Putnam Road).
- Go straight and stay on main road for 2.9 miles to crossroads and stop sign (Route 21, Liberty Highway). Two roads turn right on this stretch, but curve left on the main road at both intersections.

The short ride turns right onto Route 21.

- Straight for 1.6 miles to stop sign (Route 12 is on left and straight ahead).
- Straight for 0.9 mile to end (Route 44), in Putnam.
- Left for 0.6 mile to Sabin Street on right, immediately after small bridge.
- Right for 1.4 miles to crossroads and stop sign (Harrisville Road on right, Tripp Road on left).
- Straight for 0.2 mile to fork (Dupre Road bears right).
- Bear left and stay on main road for 0.5 mile to crossroads (Underwood Road on left, Butts Road on right).
- Right for 1.1 miles to end (Route 171). You'll see the buildings of the Hyde School, a coeducational preparatory school, on your left near the end.
- Left for 1.5 miles to where the main road curves left and Academy Road goes straight, at top of hill, in Woodstock.

Here the ride goes straight, but if you curve left you'll immediately see the Bowen House on your left.

- Straight for 0.3 mile to stop sign (merge right downhill). For a stunning view, turn right just before the stop sign into parking lot, and ride alongside the brick academic building on your right.
- Bear right for 1.2 miles to stop sign (merge left on Roseland Park Road, unmarked).
- Bear left for 0.3 mile to fork (Paine District Road bears right, Dugg Hill Road bears left).

- Bear left for 2.7 miles to second crossroads and stop sign (Chandler School Road). It comes up suddenly while you're going downhill.
- Right for 1.2 miles to stop sign at bottom of hill (merge left).
- Bear left (*Caution* here) for 0.2 mile to Fabyan Road on right.
- Right for 5.3 miles to end. You'll climb several short, steep hills.
- Left for 1.3 miles to traffic light (Route 12).
- Straight for 1.8 miles to crossroads and stop sign at top of hill, in Thompson.
- Straight for 0.4 mile to Gawron Road on right, immediately after Sunset Hill Road on left.
- Right for 1.4 miles to end (Brandy Hill Road, unmarked).
- Right for 0.3 mile to fork where O'Leary Road bears right and main road goes straight downhill.
- Straight for 1.8 miles to end (merge right at stop sign).
- Bear right for 0.6 mile to crossroads and stop sign (Quaddick Road on right, Elmwood Hill Road on left).
- Left for 1.5 miles to park entrance road on left (sharp left).

16 miles

- Follow first 4 directions of long ride.
- Right for 1.8 miles to traffic light (Route 44).
- Straight for 1.9 miles to end (merge right on Route 193).
- Right for 0.4 mile to crossroads and stop sign at top of hill, in Thompson.
- Follow last 6 directions of long ride.

Burrillville

Number of miles:	16 (26 with Pascoag extension)
Terrain:	Rolling, with some short hills. The short ride has a long, gradual hill on Route 98.
Start:	CVS Pharmacy, corner of Route 44 and Douglas Hook Road, Chepachet. It's next to the post office.
Food:	Grocery stores and small restaurants in the mill villages.

On this ride you'll explore the northwestern corner of Rhode Island, a fascinating area of woods, ponds, and mill villages tucked in valleys along swift-moving streams. Bicycling is fun on the numerous back roads that twist through the forest from one village to the next. The town of Burrillville contains seven distinct communities, all of which you'll pass through if you take the longer ride.

The ride starts from Chepachet, a town in Glocester just south of the Burrillville line, containing some handsome early nineteenth-century homes and several antiques shops. At the very beginning, you pass the Brown & Hopkins Country Store, which has been in continuous operation since 1809. Just ahead is Old Chepachet Village, a combination gift shop, restaurant, and natural-foods store. Head northeast on Old Route 102, which connects the four mill villages of Mapleville, Oakland, Glendale, and Nasonville, evenly spaced about a mile apart along the Chepachet and Branch rivers. You'll have this road nearly to yourself, since almost all the traffic will be on fast, straight New Route 102.

The first community you come to, Mapleville, is the largest of the four. Its houses, closely spaced along the road, comprise a

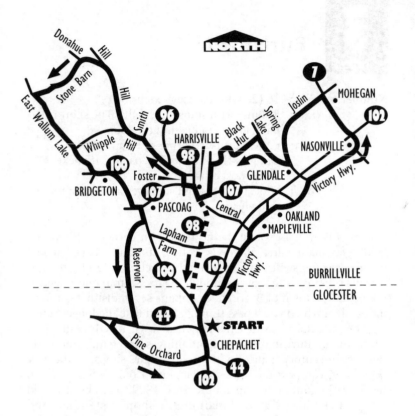

NORTH

Donahue

Hill

Stone Barn

East Wallum Lake

Whipple Hill

Smith

96

HARRISVILLE

98

100

Foster

107

BRIDGETON

PASCOAG

107

Central

98

Lapham Farm

Reservoir

100

102

Victory Hwy.

44

Pine Orchard

START

CHEPACHET

102

44

102

Black Hut

Spring Lake

Joslin

7

MOHEGAN

102

NASONVILLE

GLENDALE

Victory Hwy.

OAKLAND

MAPLEVILLE

BURRILLVILLE

GLOCESTER

HOW to get there

Exit west from I–295 onto Route 44.

Pharmacy is about 9 miles ahead on right.

- Right out of parking lot for 0.2 mile to fork where Route 102 bears right.
- Bear right and just ahead bear right again (still Route 102). Go 0.9 mile to unmarked road on right, midway up hill (Old Route 102, Victory Highway).
- Right for 1.7 miles to fork with garage in middle (main road bears left).
- Bear left for 0.4 mile to another fork where main road goes straight, in Mapleville.
- Straight (don't bear left) for 1.8 miles to another fork (sign points right to Route 7).
- Bear right over small bridge for 0.9 mile to end (Route 7), blinking light at bottom of hill.
- Bear left for 0.3 mile to traffic light (Route 102). *Caution:* Bumpy at beginning.
- Straight for 0.8 mile to crossroads (Joslin Road). You'll go through Mohegan.
- Left for 1.2 miles to Spring Lake Road, which turns sharply right while going down steep hill.
- Sharp right for 1.3 miles to Black Hut Road (unmarked) on left, which passes between two stone pillars.
- Turn left. After 1 mile the main road curves 90 degrees left. Continue 0.6 mile to end, at stop sign.
- Left for 0.6 mile to end (Route 107).
- Right for 0.1 mile to end (Main Street, Route 98), in Harrisville. Here the short ride turns left.
- Right and just ahead left on Route 107 (Chapel Street). Go 0.3 mile to second crossroads (Foster Street).
- Right for 0.1 mile to end (Route 96).
- Turn left. After 0.25 mile Route 96 turns right, but go straight for 0.4 mile to fork where Smith Road turns right and Hill Road bears left.
- Bear left for 0.7 mile to fork where Whipple Road bears left and Hill Road bears right.

- Bear right (still Hill Road). Stay on main road for 1.4 miles to another fork where Hill Road goes straight and Stone Barn Road bears left.
- Bear left on Stone Barn Road for 0.4 mile to another fork (Donahue Road bears right).
- Bear slightly left (still Stone Barn Road) for 0.7 mile to end (East Wallum Lake Road, unmarked).
- Left for 2.3 miles to end (merge left onto Route 100). *Caution:* Occasional potholes.
- Bear left for 0.9 mile to end, at stop sign.
- Left and just ahead right on Route 100. Go 0.2 mile to Reservoir Road on right.
- Right for 2.4 miles to end (Route 44).
- Right for 0.5 mile to Pine Orchard Road, a narrow lane that bears left.
- Bear left for 0.1 mile to unmarked road that turns sharply left.
- Sharp left (still Pine Orchard Road). Stay on main road for 2.9 miles to end (Route 44). Pine Orchard Road becomes Chestnut Hill Road.
- Left for 0.3 mile to parking lot on right.

16 miles

- Follow first 13 directions of long ride to Route 98.
- Left for 0.2 mile to fork (Route 98 bears right).
- Bear right for 1.3 miles to crossroads and stop sign (Lapham Farm Road).
- Straight for 1.1 miles to end (Route 100).
- Left for 0.9 mile to end (merge left on Route 44).
- Bear left (*Caution* here) for 0.2 mile to parking lot on left.

---

fascinating mixture of architectural styles, ranging from traditional mill-village duplexes with peaked roofs to rambling homes with broad porches. There are two fine churches, the first one of stone, and the second one of both stone and wood. The next three villages are smaller and more run down, with rows of identical wooden houses, originally built for the workers, flanking the stone or redbrick mills. In Nasonville, the Western Hotel, a marvelous, long wooden building with a porch along its entire front, guards the corner of Old Route 102 and Route 7. There's a good restaurant in the building. Across the street is a former Victorian schoolhouse with a bell tower, tastefully remodeled into apartments.

Turn northwest on Route 7 and pass through Mohegan, with its row of mill houses in varying need of repair straggling up the hillside. The route now heads west along narrow wooded roads toward Harrisville, the most attractive of Burrillville's communities. You'll pass Spring Lake, nestled in the woods and flanked by a cluster of summer cottages. A small beach here is a good spot for a swim. As you arrive in Harrisville, you'll see a beautiful dam and a complex of nineteenth-century brick and stone mills. A traditional white New England church stands above the dam and millpond, and in the next block is another stately church, this one of brick. The short ride now heads back to Chepachet along Route 98, a smooth secondary road that passes through a stretch of open fields.

The long ride heads northwest along narrow lanes to a very rural area. Small farms with rustic barns and stone walls punctuate the wooded hillsides. Descend to the Wilson Reservoir and arrive in Bridgeton, where there's a wonderful red wooden schoolhouse with a graceful bell tower. Bridgeton blends into Pascoag, the largest of Burrillville's villages. Just out of town you'll enjoy a relaxing ride along the slender Pascoag Reservoir. The last 2 miles are mostly downhill as you wind along a small wooded lane with two ponds.

The Northern Border Ride
Slatersville–Uxbridge–Millville–Mendon–Blackstone

Number of miles:	11 (26 with Massachusetts loop)
Terrain:	Rolling, with several short hills.
Start:	Slatersville Plaza, junction of Routes 5, 102, and 146A in North Smithfield, Rhode Island, near the Massachusetts line.
Food:	Grocery in Millville (26-mile ride). Lowell's Restaurant, Route 16, Mendon (26-mile ride). Excellent ice cream and fish and chips. Wright's Farm (great fried chicken), 0.6 mile off route on Inman Road. There's a coffee shop in the shopping center at the end.

The region just west and northwest of Woonsocket, straddling the center of Rhode Island's northern border, is ideal for bicycling. Here is the rural New England of Currier-and-Ives prints, with narrow wooded lanes meandering alongside stone walls, cozy log cabins nestled amid pine groves, and unspoiled small towns. The long ride passes within a half mile of Southwick's Zoo, a large collection of animals from all over the world.

The ride starts a half mile south of the Massachusetts border and soon passes through the lovely mill village of Slatersville. The triangular green is framed by a traditional white New England church and gracious homes dating from around 1810. Just ahead is the dignified town hall with tall white pillars. Across the road, a complex of Victorian stone and brick mills lies in the steep valley of the Branch River.

A mile out of town is an impressive two-tiered dam on your left. Head west, just below the state line, along untraveled back roads that bob up and down short wooded hills. The route turns north on Ironmine Road, which crosses the state line into Uxbridge, Massachusetts. Turn east, following more narrow country lanes just north of the Rhode Island border. It's mostly downhill to the valley of the Blackstone River, where you cross Route 146A.

Just ahead parallel the river and arrive in Millville, a mill town that has seen better days. Just after you turn away from the river on the short ride toward Rhode Island, you pass a handsome stone church standing proudly above the town. Next to the church is a parking lot with a sign that says MILLVILLE LOCK. I followed an abandoned railroad for a mile to a dangerously exposed bridge over the Blackstone River, but I saw no sign of a lock. From here, it's 1.5 miles back to the starting point.

The long ride heads farther north into Massachusetts, making a loop that begins and ends in Millville. A mile out of town you pass the Chestnut Hill Meeting House, a simple, white wooden church built in 1769. After another mile, Vineyard Street is on your left. Here the ride continues straight ahead, but you may turn left for a half mile to visit Southwick's Zoo.

When you come to Route 16, you have a fine view to your right from the top of a ridge before you reach the hilltop town of Mendon. When you leave Route 16, the parking lot for Lowell's Restaurant will be on your left. This is a great rest stop, with superb ice cream and fish and chips. Just beyond is a graceful white church and the old town hall. Leaving Mendon, ascend a small ridge with a beautiful view on your left and then enjoy a long, lazy descent back into Millville, where you rejoin the short ride for the brief stretch across the Rhode Island border to Slatersville.

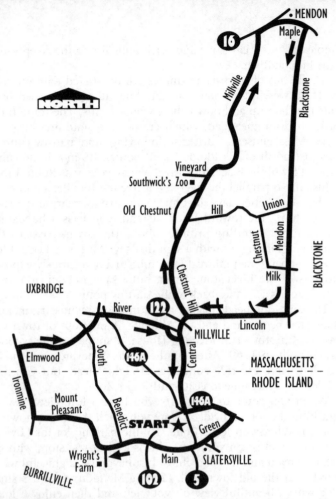

NORTH

MENDON
Maple
16
Millville
Blackstone
Vineyard
Southwick's Zoo ■
Old Chestnut
Hill
Union
Chestnut
Mendon
BLACKSTONE
Milk
UXBRIDGE
River
122
Chestnut Hill
MILLVILLE
Lincoln
Elmwood
South
146A
Central
MASSACHUSETTS
RHODE ISLAND
Ironmine
Mount Pleasant
Benedict
146A
START ★
Green
Wright's Farm ■
Main
SLATERSVILLE
BURRILLVILLE
102
5

HOW to get there
From the south, take the Forestdale-Slatersville exit from Route 146. Turn right at the end of the exit ramp, then immediately left at end, and go 1.5 miles to parking lot on left, just past the traffic light.

From the north, head south on Route 146 to the Route 146A, North Smithfield exit. Turn left at end of ramp for 1.3 miles to parking lot on right, just past the traffic light.

- Right out of parking lot on Route 102, and just ahead go straight at traffic light onto Route 146A. Go 0.7 mile to Green Street on right, just before traffic light.
- Right for 1.7 miles to Route 102, at traffic light. You'll go through Slatersville.
- Go straight and stay on main road for 2.5 miles to end (Ironmine Road). The first left, Inman Road, leads 0.6 mile to Wright's Farm—great fried chicken!
- Right for 1.4 miles to Elmwood Street on right.
- Right for 1.9 miles to second crossroads (Balm of Life Spring Road), just after you go under Route 146. Notice old cement milepost on far left corner.
- Right for 0.1 mile to crossroads and stop sign (Route 146A).
- Straight for 1 mile to fork (West Street bears right).
- Bear right for 0.4 mile to end (Central Street, in Millville). Here the short ride turns right.
- Left for 0.3 mile to traffic light (Route 122). *Caution:* Metal-grate bridge at bottom of hill is very slippery when wet; walk your bike.
- Straight and immediately left on Chestnut Hill Road. Stay on main road for 6.2 miles to end (merge right on Route 16). Southwick's Zoo is on left after 2.5 miles (0.5 mile down Vineyard Street).
- Bear right for 0.2 mile to fork where Maple Street bears right downhill (sign says TO BELLINGHAM).
- Bear right for 0.2 mile to stop sign. The back entrance to Lowell's Restaurant is on your left at the beginning (*Caution:* Speed bump).
- Bear right downhill for 0.1 mile to Blackstone Street on right.
- Right for 5.5 miles, staying on main road, to second crossroads and stop sign (Lincoln Street). School on left corner. *Caution:* Bumpy sections.
- Right for 0.9 mile to fork (Depraitre Street bears right).
- Bear slightly left downhill on main road for 0.9 mile to traffic

light (Route 122).
- Straight for 1.5 miles to stop sign (merge left on Route 146A). *Caution* again on metal-grate bridge.
- Bear left for 0.2 mile to parking lot on right, just past traffic light.

11 miles

- Follow first 8 directions of long ride, to Central Street in Millville.
- Right for 1.2 miles to stop sign (merge left on Route 146A).
- Bear left for 0.2 mile to parking lot on right, just past traffic light.

5 Smithfield–North Smithfield–Slatersville

Number of miles: 13 (27 with Stillwater–Georgiaville–Esmond extension)

Terrain: Rolling, with one tough hill and lots of short, steep ones. The long ride has two additional hills.

Start: Small shopping center at junction of Route 5 and Log Road, Smithfield.

Food: None on the short ride. Restaurant and country store in Nasonville. Wright's Farm (all-you-can-eat fried chicken; a true feast) just off route near Nasonville. Restaurant on Route 102. Pizza at end. McDonald's and Burger King at corner of Routes 5 and 44, 2 miles south of starting point.

The region northwest of Providence, midway between the city and the Massachusetts border, abounds with twisting secondary roads that provide enjoyable bicycling if you're willing to tackle lots of little hills and an occasional big one. The landscape is primarily rolling woodland dotted with boulders, ponds, and picturesque mill villages. At several spots along the route, tumbling streams rush alongside or underneath the road.

Begin the ride in Smithfield, a town blending undeveloped woods and farmland, apple orchards, old mill villages, and some pockets of suburban growth. After leaving the parking lot, immediately follow Log Road along the shore of the unspoiled Woonasquatucket Reservoir (also called the Stillwater Reservoir or Stump Pond). Continue

for several miles along Log Road, a beckoning byway that seems to have been designed with bicyclists in mind. Two more narrow lanes bring you past three small dams and pristine Tarkiln Pond to Route 7.

The short ride turns southeast back toward the starting point on Route 7, an excellent cycling road that bobs up and down small wooded hills and then plunges steeply in a thrilling descent. To finish, you'll cross the cascading Woonasquatucket River and once again go along the reservoir on Log Road, this time in the opposite direction.

The long ride heads north into Nasonville, a mill village (part of the town of Burrillville) that is best known for Wright's Farm, a large restaurant famous for fried chicken. Side roads provide views of Slatersville Reservoir and an impressive two-tiered dam on your right. A mile ahead is Slatersville, the finest traditional mill village in Rhode Island, with most of its buildings dating back to the early 1800s. The handsome, pillared town hall and a lovely white church standing above a triangular green are just off the route. A cluster of Victorian stone and brick mills lies below in the steep valley of the Branch River.

A steady climb out of Slatersville heads toward Route 104, which eventually leads to the opposite shore of the Woonasquatucket Reservoir. A mile ahead, turn onto a narrow side road that descends steeply into Stillwater, a lovely and classic mill village. Most of the stately wooden houses have been restored, but unfortunately the old brick mill was a victim of fire. Just ahead is the Smith-Appleby House, built in 1696. Pedal into Georgiaville, another fine mill village, with three-story wood and stone houses and a large brick mill tastefully recycled into condominiums. A small beach on Georgiaville Pond is a good spot for a swim or rest. Near the end of the ride you'll have a steady climb on Route 104 followed by a fast descent to the shore of the Woonasquatucket Reservoir.

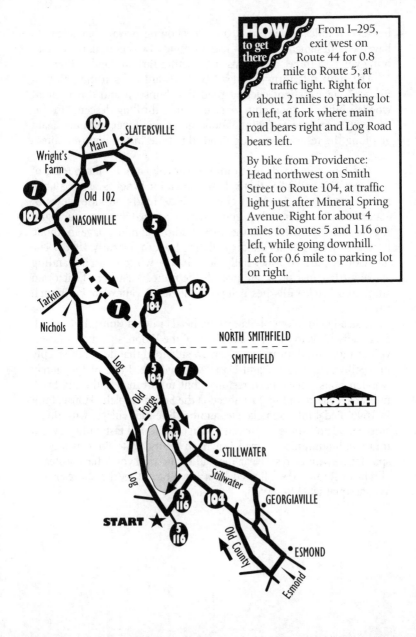

HOW to get there
From I–295, exit west on Route 44 for 0.8 mile to Route 5, at traffic light. Right for about 2 miles to parking lot on left, at fork where main road bears right and Log Road bears left.

By bike from Providence: Head northwest on Smith Street to Route 104, at traffic light just after Mineral Spring Avenue. Right for about 4 miles to Routes 5 and 116 on left, while going downhill. Left for 0.6 mile to parking lot on right.

102
SLATERSVILLE
Main
Wright's Farm
7
Old 102
102
NASONVILLE
5
104
Tarkin
7
5
104
Nichols

NORTH SMITHFIELD
SMITHFIELD

NORTH

Log
Old Forge
5
104
7

5
104
116
STILLWATER
Stillwater
GEORGIAVILLE
Log
5
116
104
START ★
5
116
Old County
ESMOND
Esmond

DIREC-TIONS for the ride

27 miles

■ Left out of parking lot on Log Road (don't get on Route 5). Go 0.2 mile to fork (Mann School Road bears left).

■ Bear right (still Log Road, unmarked) for 1.3 miles to Old Forge Road, which bears right. Here the ride goes straight, but if you wish to do only the Stillwater–Georgiaville–Esmond section of the ride (11 miles) bear right for 0.5 mile to Route 5, at stop sign. Turn right for 1.2 miles to Route 116 North on left. Follow last 10 directions of long ride, beginning "Left for 0.6 mile . . ."

■ Straight (still Log Road) for 3.9 miles to end (merge left on Nichols Road). There are six short, steep hills on the first half of this section.

■ Bear left for 0.3 mile to end (Tarkiln Road). Notice small dam on left at bottom of hill.

■ Right for 1 mile to end (Route 7), staying on main road. You'll pass a small dam on your right and another one on your left. At the end the short ride turns right.

■ Left for 1 mile to blinking light where Route 7 bears right across small bridge, in Nasonville. The Western Hotel is a good spot for a snack.

■ Bear right and just ahead turn right on Old Route 102 (unmarked). Go 0.25 mile to Nasonville Road, which bears right.

■ Bear right for 0.2 mile to end (merge right on Old Route 102).

■ Bear right for 0.2 mile to Old Nasonville Road, which bears right. Here the ride bears right, but to go to Wright's Farm curve left for 50 yards to Route 102, and straight for 0.1 mile.

■ Bear right for 0.25 mile to end (Route 102).

■ Right for 0.6 mile to traffic light.

■ Right for 1 mile to Route 5, which bears right. You'll pass a two-tiered dam on your right after 0.2 mile; it's worth stopping for a look. The ride bears right on Route 5, but it's worth going straight for 200 yards to see the lovely church and green in Slatersville.

- Bear right for 3.6 miles to traffic light (Route 104). Notice the dam on your right at the beginning as you cross the Branch River.
- Right for 1.3 miles to end (merge left on Route 7).
- Bear left (*Caution* here) for 0.2 mile to where Routes 5 and 104 bear right.
- Bear right for 1.3 miles to crossroads (Old Forge Road, unmarked, on right).
  Here the ride goes straight, but you can shorten the distance to 19 miles by following the last 2 directions of the short ride.
- Straight for 1.3 miles to Route 116 on left.
- Left for 0.6 mile to small crossroads while going downhill (John Mowry Road on left, Stillwater Road on right).
- Right for 1.6 miles to stop sign where Stillwater Road turns right. You'll ride through Stillwater.
- Turn right and just ahead curve left on main road. Go 0.6 mile to unmarked road that bears right down a short hill, in Georgiaville.
- Bear right and walk across the pedestrian bridge. Go less than 0.2 mile to fork (Homestead Avenue bears left).
- Bear right and just ahead bear right again at another fork. Go 0.1 mile to end (Route 104).
  Here the ride turns left, but you can cut 2 miles off the route by turning right for 1.7 miles to Route 116 South on left (notice octagonal house on left after 0.2 mile), and left (*Caution* here) for 0.6 mile to starting point on right.
- Left for 0.8 mile to Esmond Street on right.
- Right for 0.4 mile to crossroads and stop sign, passing through Esmond.
- Turn right and immediately curve right on main road (Old County Road). Go 1.5 miles to crossroads and stop sign (Route 104).
- Left for 1.2 miles to Route 116 South (Pleasant View Avenue) on left, while going downhill.
- Turn left (*Caution* here—busy intersection) and go 0.6 mile to parking lot on right.

13 miles

- Follow first 5 directions of long ride, to Route 7.
- Right for 3 miles to fork where Route 7 goes straight and Routes 5 and 104 bear right.
- Bear right for 1.3 miles to crossroads (Old Forge Road, unmarked, on right).
- Right for 0.5 mile to end (merge left on Log Road).
- Bear left for 1.5 miles to starting point on right.

Lincoln Loop

Number of miles:	15
Terrain:	Rolling, with lots of short, steep hills.
Start:	Wake Robin Medical Center, Route 116 in Lincoln, just west of Route 146. It's across from Lincoln Mall.
Food:	Snack bar on Route 246 near Lincoln Woods. Wendy's at end.

Lincoln, an affluent town just northwest of Providence, is ideal for cycling. Its many back roads wind past horse farms, country estates, and attractive houses nestled in the woods. A section of this ride passes through Lincoln Woods, a state park with a beach on Olney Pond. (The beach is just off the route, but Ride 7 goes right by it.) Most of Lincoln is not densely populated, and traffic on the secondary roads is pleasantly light.

The ride begins with a descent on Route 246, a lightly traveled road that runs parallel to busy Route 146. After turning past a limestone quarry, you'll ascend onto a ridge to the gracious hamlet of Lime Rock, where you'll pass an old brick Masonic hall and the Mowry Tavern, a long, wide-porched building that dates from 1686. It is now a private home. Just ahead, enjoy a long, exhilarating descent past well-manicured horse farms on Great Road. The handsome old buildings along this road have earned it the status of a State Historic District. Turn onto Route 123 and follow the Moshassuck River, a small stream, past gracious old houses, gentleman farms, and small dams to the entrance to Lincoln Woods.

Lincoln Woods is a park that Rhode Islanders can be proud of. In 1981 the park, which had become shabby and neglected, received a complete face-lift—the roads were repaved, grass was replanted, and the beach received a new bathhouse and layer of sand. Lincoln Woods is a pleasure to bike through once you climb the steep hill to the pond.

Shortly after leaving the park you'll pass Lincoln Greyhound Park, which was originally a raceway for horses. Head north back toward the starting point on Angell Road, another pleasant side road curving past horse farms and well-kept houses secluded on large wooded lots. Near the end of the ride you'll pass North Central State Airport, a small facility used for flying lessons, sightseeing flights, and storage of private planes. There's a good view if you turn onto the main entrance road for 100 yards. Finish with a long, steady descent back to the starting point.

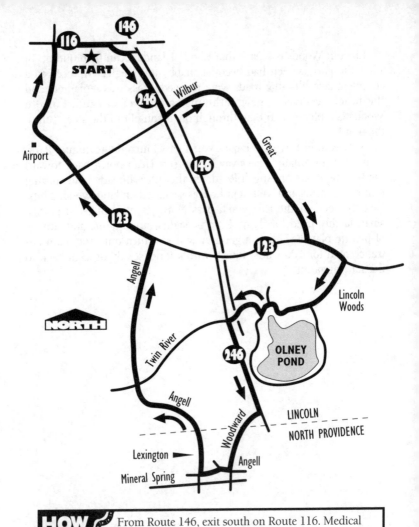

HOW to get there

From Route 146, exit south on Route 116. Medical center is just ahead on left at traffic light.

By bike from Providence, head north on Charles Street. Cross Mineral Spring Avenue (Route 15) and continue for about 3 miles to second traffic light (Route 123). Turn left for about 3.5 miles to traffic light (Route 116). Turn right for 0.4 mile to medical center on right, at second traffic light.

- Right on Route 116 for 0.2 mile to entrance ramp to Route 146 South.
- Bear right for 0.2 mile to Route 246, which bears right just before Route 146.
- Bear right for 0.6 mile to crossroads (Wilbur Road, unmarked).
- Left for 2.5 miles to end (Route 123). Wilbur Road becomes Great Road.
- Left for 0.5 mile to entrance to Lincoln Woods on right.
- Right for 1.1 miles to fork where main road bears left. There may be a poster about Zachariah Allen, an early local forester, at the fork.
- Bear left for 0.1 mile to park exit road on right, at traffic island. Here the ride turns right, but if you wish you may continue straight and loop counterclockwise around Olney Pond, returning to this same intersection after 2.3 miles. You'll pass the beach after 0.5 mile.
- Right for 0.6 mile to traffic light (Route 246, Old Louisquisset Pike).
- Left for 1.2 miles to Woodward Road on right.
- Turn right. Just ahead bear left on main road for 0.7 mile to small crossroads (Angell Road, unmarked) just before traffic light.
- Right for 0.1 mile to fork.
- Bear left downhill for 0.25 mile to crossroads and stop sign (Lexington Avenue, unmarked).
- Right for 1.8 miles to crossroads and stop sign (Twin River Road, unmarked). Lexington Avenue becomes Angell Road.
- Go straight. Stay on main road for 1.7 miles to end (Route 123).
- Left for 2.6 miles to Route 116, at traffic light.
- Right for almost 0.4 mile to parking lot on right, at second traffic light.

Blackstone Valley Tour
Lincoln–Cumberland

Number of miles:	16 (27 with Cumberland loop). Optional loop around Lincoln Woods adds 3.7 miles to either ride.
Terrain:	Hilly. To reward your efforts, however, there are several exciting descents.
Start:	Wake Robin Medical Center, Route 116 in Lincoln, just west of Route 146. It's across from Lincoln Mall.
Food:	Restaurant in Berkeley. Convenience store in Cumberland Hill. Grocery in Albion. Burger King on Route 122 in Cumberland. Wendy's at end.

This ride explores a fascinating region that formed part of Rhode Island's industrial heartland during the nineteenth century. Lying midway between Providence and Woonsocket, the area is far enough from the two cities to be primarily rural, except for the string of small mill villages nestled along the Blackstone River. Between the villages, you'll ascend onto ridges and then drop down to the riverbank. A highlight of the ride is a 2-mile stretch along the new Blackstone Valley Bikeway, which threads between the river on one side and the 170-year-old Blackstone Canal on the other. A scenic optional loop makes a circuit of Lincoln Woods State Park.

Lincoln, an attractive suburban community on the south bank of the Blackstone, is the starting point of the ride. You head east for about 2 miles, enjoying a long, smooth descent to the Blackstone River. You'll cross the river into Cumberland over a high bridge that provides a dramatic view of the mill village of Ashton. Just ahead

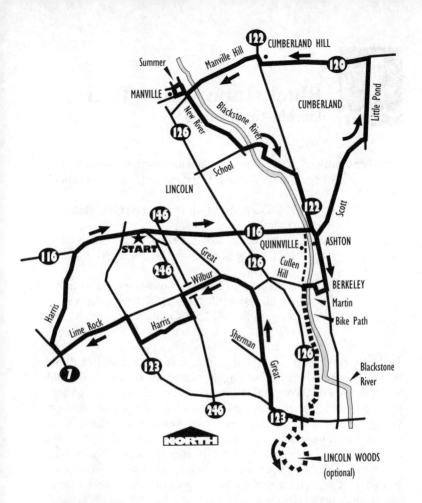

HOW to get there

From Route 146, exit south on Route 116. Plaza is just ahead on left at traffic light.

By bike from Providence, head north on Charles Street. Cross Mineral Spring Avenue (Route 15) and continue for about 3 miles to second traffic light (Route 123). Turn left for about 3.5 miles to traffc light (Route 116). Turn right for 0.4 mile to plaza on right, at second traffic light.

- Right on Route 116 for 2.3 miles to end (Route 122, Mendon Road). Spectacular view from right side of bridge over Blackstone River just before end.
- Right for 50 yards to Scott Road on left, at blinking light. Here the short ride goes straight.
- Left (*Caution* here) for 2.3 miles to stop sign where main road curves left.
- Curve left for 1.2 miles to end (Route 120, Nate Whipple Highway).
- Left for 2.3 miles to end (Route 122, Mendon Road).
- Right and just ahead left at traffic light on Manville Hill Road. Go 0.7 mile to another light at bottom of long hill.
  You will now make a short clockwise loop through the unique mill village of Manville and return to this intersection after 0.4 mile.
- Right for 100 yards to first left, Spring Street. Notice dam on right.
- Left for 100 yards to first right (Fall Street), right for one short block to crossroads, right for one block to end, and right for 0.1 mile back to traffic light.
- Straight for 1.7 miles to crossroads and blinking light (School Street), in Albion.
- Left (*Caution* here) for 0.9 mile to end (Route 122, Mendon Road), at traffic light. *Caution:* Steep, curving descent with railroad tracks at bottom.
- Right for 1 mile to Store Hill Road on right, just after traffic light where Angell Road turns left. You will now make a short clockwise loop through Ashton and return to this intersection after 0.3 mile.
- Right for 0.1 mile to end (Front Street), right for one block to first right (Webber Street), right for 0.1 mile to crossroads, and left for 50 yards to end (Route 122).
- Right for 0.8 mile to crossroads after traffic light (Barrett Street on left, Gray Street on right). Davenport's Restaurant, on your right immediately after the light, is excellent.
- Right for 0.1 mile to second right (Woodward Street), in Berkeley.
- Right for less than 0.2 mile to end (Martin Street, unmarked).

- Left for 0.4 mile to Blackstone Valley Bikeway, which crosses the road immediately after bridge over Blackstone River.

    Here the ride turns left, but if you turn right for 0.7 mile you'll come to the future Blackstone River State Park visitors center. A footpath continues beyond it for 0.2 mile to an impressive dam across the river.

- Turn left on bikeway, which runs between the Blackstone Canal on your right and the river on your left. After 1.6 miles the bike path turns right across the canal and widens into a road. Continue 0.4 mile to end (Route 123, Front Street), passing grim brick mills on your left.

- Right for 1.4 miles to Great Road on right. It's 0.7 mile beyond second traffic light. A striking modern church is on your right at the first light, and the Eleazer Arnold House is on your right just after the second light.

    The entrance to Lincoln Woods State Park is on your left just beyond the Arnold House. To do the optional loop through the park, turn left and stay on main road for 3 miles to end, at stop sign. You'll climb steeply and ride counterclockwise around Olney Pond. Then turn right for 0.7 mile to end (Route 123 again), and left for 0.5 mile to Great Road on right.

- Right for 0.7 mile to fork (Sherman Avenue bears left, main road bears right).

- Bear right for 1.3 miles to another fork (Great Road bears right, Wilbur Road bears left). You'll climb a long, steady hill and go through the hamlet of Lime Rock just before the fork.

- Bear left for 0.4 mile to crossroads and stop sign (Route 246, Louisquisset Pike).

- Left for 0.5 mile to Harris Avenue on right.

- Right for 0.9 mile to end (Route 123, Jenckes Hill Road). This is a gradual climb.

- Right for 0.4 mile to crossroads (Wilbur Road on right, Lime Rock Road on left).

    Here the ride turns left, but you can cut 2.7 miles off the route by continuing straight for 2.7 miles to traffic light (Route 116), and

then right for almost 0.4 mile to medical center on right, at second traffic light.
- Left for 1.6 miles to crossroads and stop sign (Route 7, Douglas Pike).
- Right for 0.2 mile to Harris Road on right.
- Right for 1.7 mile to crossroads and stop sign (Route 116). Most of this stretch is a gradual climb.
- Right for 1.4 miles to medical center on right, at third traffic light.

16 miles

- Follow first direction of long ride.
- Right for 0.2 mile to Store Hill Road on right, just after traffic light. You will now make a short clockwise loop through Ashton and return to this intersection after 0.3 mile.
- Follow last 17 directions of long ride, beginning "Right for 0.1 mile to end (Front Street) . . ."

---

you'll ride through Ashton and then Berkeley, two attractive mill villages (both part of Cumberland) set back a block or two from the main road. Their orderly rows of identical brick duplexes seem transplanted from England during the Industrial Revolution.

Just beyond Berkeley you'll cross the Blackstone River again back into Lincoln and ride for two miles on the bikeway that runs between the river and the parallel Blackstone Canal. The canal, which connected Providence with Worcester, was opened in 1828. It closed twenty years later, unable to compete with the railroad, which could carry much larger payloads at greatly increased speed. The bikeway is part of Blackstone Valley State Park, a 19-mile linear historical park that is under construction along the river.

About a mile farther on you'll pass the Eleazer Arnold House, built around 1687 and noteworthy for its massive stone chimney. Just ahead is the entrance to Lincoln Woods State Park. If you wish, you can make a hilly, 3.7-mile side trip into the park and around Olney

Pond, where you'll pass a swimming area. The ride turns north onto Great Road, a "great" road for biking that climbs gradually past horse farms to the unspoiled hamlet of Lime Rock. Several handsome old buildings have given this road the designation of a State Historic District. You'll pass the Mowry Tavern, a long building with a wide porch. It dates from 1686 and is now a private residence. The Conklin Limestone Quarry, which is the oldest continuously operated quarry in the country (it dates from 1840), is at the far end of the village. Shortly before the end are two gradual climbs, with a glorious descent through farmland between them.

The long ride loops north through Cumberland. After heading away from the river for several miles, a screaming descent brings you back into the valley and across the river to Manville (part of Lincoln), the largest of the mill towns on the ride. Here brick rowhouses and three- and four-story wooden tenements with wide front porches cling to the steep hillside. Follow the valley for 2 miles into Albion, another old mill village within the town of Lincoln. The mill has recently been remodeled into condominiums. Just ahead you'll cross the Blackstone again back into Cumberland, and after 2 miles you'll rejoin the short ride just before Ashton.

Cumberland–
Wrentham–Plainville

Number of miles:	18 (29 with Plainville loop, 10 with shortcut)
Terrain:	Rolling to hilly, with two long descents on the 29-mile ride.
Start:	Diamond Hill State Park, Route 114, Cumberland.
Food:	Country store at corner of Route 121 and Hancock Street, Wrentham. Burger King, corner of Routes 106 and 152, Plainville (0.3 mile off route of 29-mile ride). Dunkin' Donuts between Routes 1 and 1A in North Attleboro (29-mile ride). Ice cream at end opposite entrance to park.

This ride explores the rural, largely wooded area surrounding the northeast corner of the state. You can amble along at a leisurely pace to savor the beauty of the narrow, twisting back roads. Near the end you'll enjoy a delightful ride along the Diamond Hill Reservoir.

The route starts from Diamond Hill State Park, marked by a cliff of veined quartz over 200 feet high, a favorite spot for rock climbers. The park once contained a ski area, but the unpredictable snowfall of the Rhode Island winter made its continued operation unprofitable. The first few miles of the ride climb gradually on Route 120, passing Sneech Pond. You will be rewarded with a smooth descent on West Wrentham Road through open farmland with fine views.

About 7 miles from the starting point you cross the state line into Wrentham, Massachusetts, a gracious town of small farms, horse pastures, and well-maintained homes. Although technically within the Boston metropolitan area, the community is far enough from the city to have a rural, rather than suburban, atmosphere. Spring Street, a narrow winding lane, bobs up and over several sharp hills, none long

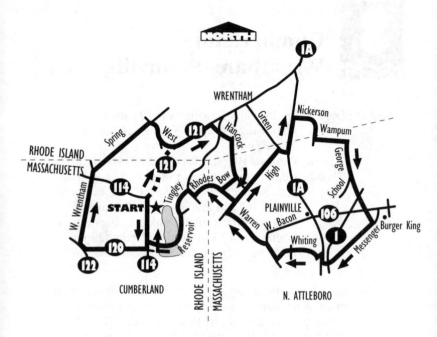

NORTH

WRENTHAM

Nickerson

Wampum

Spring

West

121

Hancock

Green

RHODE ISLAND

MASSACHUSETTS

121

Rhodes Bow

High

George

School

114

Tingley

1A

PLAINVILLE

106

W. Wrentham

START

Reservoir

Warren

W. Bacon

Burger King

Messenger

120

Whiting

1

122

114

RHODE ISLAND

MASSACHUSETTS

CUMBERLAND

N. ATTLEBORO

HOW to get there

From I–295, exit north on Route 114 and go about 4 miles to parking lot on right.

By bike from Providence, head north on North Main Street. At Pawtucket line bear left on Route 122 (Main Street). Follow Route 122 for about 5 miles to Marshall Avenue on right. Right for 0.6 mile to end (Route 114). Left for about 6 miles to parking lot on right.

- Left on Route 114 for 1.4 miles to traffic light (Route 120, Nate Whipple Highway). *Note:* 10-mile ride turns right on Route 114 instead of left.
- Right for 2.5 miles to end (Route 122, Mendon Road).
- Right for 0.2 mile to West Wrentham Road on right, at traffic light.

- Right for 2.4 miles to traffic light (Route 114, Pine Swamp Road).
- Straight and just ahead bear slightly right at fork. Go 2 miles to crossroads and stop sign (West Street, unmarked). *Caution:* Sandy spots.
- Right for 0.9 mile to end (Route 121).
- Left for 1.2 miles to Hancock Street on right (country store on corner).
- Right for 0.7 mile to end, at top of hill.
- Right (still Hancock Street, unmarked) for 1.1 miles to Bow Street, a small lane on right (sign may say TO WENTWORTH).
- Right for 0.5 mile to end (Rhodes Street, unmarked). Here the 18-mile ride turns right.
- Left for 0.6 mile to end (High Street, unmarked).
- Left for 1.4 miles to end, at stop sign.
- Right for 0.2 mile to end (Route 1A).
- Left for 0.7 mile to Nickerson Street on right, just after traffic light.
- Right for 0.7 mile to Wampum Street on left.
- Turn left and stay on main road for 1.9 miles to Route 1, at stop sign.
- Straight for 0.5 mile to Route 106. Here the ride goes straight, but to go to Burger King turn left for 0.3 mile. It's on your right just before traffic light, set back from road.
- Straight for 0.1 mile to end.
- Right for 1.5 miles to traffic light (Routes 1 and 1A).
- Straight across Route 1 at light, then immediately right on Route 1A. Be sure you're on Route 1A and not Route 1. Go 100 yards to Whiting Street on left.

- Left for 1.1 miles to end. (The road turns sharply and changes names several times, but stay on it to end.)
- Right for 0.3 mile to second left (Warren Street), just after country club on left.
- Left for 1.2 miles to end (High Street, unmarked).
- Right for 0.3 mile to Rhodes Street on left.
- Left for 1.3 miles to end (Burnt Swamp Road, unmarked).
- Right for 0.3 mile to end (Reservoir Road on left).
- Left for 2.5 miles to end (Route 114).
- Right for 0.9 mile to park entrance on right.

18 miles

- Follow first 10 directions of long ride to Rhodes Street.
- Right for 0.7 mile to end (Burnt Swamp Road, unmarked).
- Follow last 3 directions of long ride.

10 miles

- Right on Route 114 for 0.2 mile to traffic island (Route 121 bears right).
- Bear right for 2.8 miles to Hancock Street on right (country store on corner).
- Right for 0.7 mile to end, at top of hill.
- Right (still Hancock Street, unmarked) for 1.1 miles to Bow Street, a small lane on right (sign may say TO WENTWORTH).
- Right for 0.5 mile to end (Rhodes Street, unmarked).
- Right for 0.7 mile to end (Burnt Swamp Road, unmarked).
- Follow last 3 directions of the 29-mile ride.

---

enough to be discouraging. You can stop for a breather at the country store in Sheldonville, a village within Wrentham. Notice the stately white church on your left just past the store.

Ahead is the town of Plainville, just east of the Rhode Island border. This town is similar to Wrentham, but a little more built up. You will pass a branch of the Wentworth Institute, an engineering school whose main campus is in Boston. You cross back into Rhode Island, descend to the Diamond Hill Reservoir, and ride along the shoreline. The rugged cliffs of Diamond Hill are on your right just before the end of the ride.

An exhilarating descent on High Street in Plainville begins the loop of the long ride. At the top of the hill between Plainville and North Attleboro is the World War I Memorial Park, which has a small zoo and a great view from a fire tower, which is sometimes open on days when the forest-fire risk is low. Rejoin the short ride in time for the section along the Diamond Hill Reservoir.

South Attleboro– Cumberland–Wrentham– North Attleboro

Number of miles:	18 (28 with Wrentham extension, 12 with short-cut through Arnold Mills.)
Terrain:	Gently rolling, with one tough hill climbing up from the reservoir and two moderate hills. The long ride is rolling. The 12-mile ride has one moderate hill near the end.
Start:	Papa Gino's, South Attleboro Square, a shopping center at junction of Routes 1 and 123 in South Attleboro, Massachusetts.
Food:	Country store on Route 114 opposite Reservoir Road. Restaurant in Arnold Mills. Big Apple fruit stand and cider mill, Wrentham. Country store on corner of Route 121 and Hancock Street, Wrentham. Pizza at end.

The region straddling the Rhode Island–Massachusetts border north of Pawtucket is surprisingly rural. Its many quiet country roads are ideal for bicycling.

The ride begins in the suburban community of South Attleboro, just north of Pawtucket. The route angles northwestward into Cumberland, Rhode Island, on Mendon Road, which turns into Abbott Run Valley Road. This long road passes open hillsides and expensive houses. This part of Cumberland, called the Arnold Mills section, is considered a desirable place to live.

When you reach Route 120, the 12-mile ride turns east, and after a half mile passes through the charming village of Arnold Mills itself.

It boasts a classic New England church and a small dam. The two longer rides continue north along the Diamond Hill Reservoir, which provides Pawtucket's water supply. The reservoir lies nestled among low, forested hills.

Just past the reservoir, you climb steeply and cross back into Massachusetts in North Attleboro. The remainder of the ride is a delight as you pass large, prosperous dairy farms and then come down from the ridge on a long, lazy descent. Near the end of the ride is the Abbott Run, a stream flowing between two old stone embankments. Just before the parking lot is Fuller Memorial Hospital, a private psychiatric facility with a campuslike setting.

The long ride makes a loop through the rural, rolling countryside of Wrentham, Massachusetts. This is a gracious community on the outer fringe of the Boston metropolitan area, far enough from the city to be nearly undeveloped. The last mile of Williams Street crosses into Franklin, which in contrast to Wrentham is courting suburban growth. But soon you pedal past Wrentham's horse pastures and barns once again. Union Street ascends gradually onto a ridge with fine views; then you descend past the Big Apple, a large orchard featuring hot and cold cider, doughnuts, and freshly picked apples in season. It's a refreshing rest stop on a nippy fall day. Just ahead you nick the northeast corner of Rhode Island on Burnt Swamp Road, passing small farms bordered by forest, before rejoining the 18-mile ride.

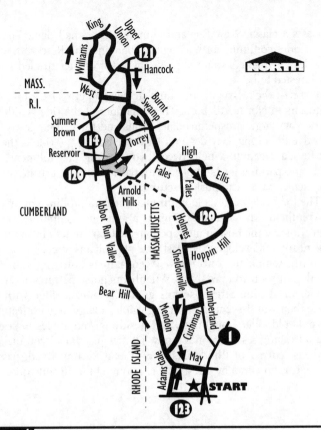

HOW to get there

From the south, exit north from I–95 onto Route 1A (the first exit in Massachusetts). Go 1 mile to Route 123 and turn left. The parking lot is just ahead on your right on the far side of Route 1.

From the northeast, exit west from I–95 onto Route 123. The parking lot is 2 miles ahead on your right.

From the west, exit south from I–295 onto Route 1. Parking lot is 2 miles ahead on your right.

By bike from Providence, head north on North Main Street. At Pawtucket line bear left on Route 122 (Main Street). Follow Route 122 for 4 miles to Route 123, then right for 3 miles to parking lot on left.

DIREC-TIONS

for the ride

28 miles

- Right out of south side of parking lot on Route 123 for 0.7 mile to Adamsdale Road on right.
- Right for 0.7 mile to end, at stop sign (May Street on right).
- Bear left on Mendon Road (unmarked) for 1.8 miles to fork (Bear Hill Road bears left uphill).
- Bear right on main road for 2.2 miles to end at Route 120. Here the 12-mile ride turns right.
- Left for 0.2 mile to traffic light (Route 114, Diamond Hill Road).
- Right for 0.6 mile to Reservoir Road on right.
- Right for 1.6 miles to fork where the main road bears left along reservoir.
- Bear left for 0.9 mile to Burnt Swamp Road on right. The main road curves left at the intersection. Here the 18-mile ride turns right.
- Curve left on main road for 0.3 mile to Sumner Brown Road on left.
- Left for 1.6 miles to end (Route 121). You'll climb several short, steep hills.
- Right for 0.8 mile to West Street (unmarked) on left, at bottom of hill.
- Left for 0.4 mile to Williams Street on right.
- Bear right for 2.4 miles to end (King Street).
- Right for 0.2 mile to Upper Union Street on right, just before I–495.
- Right for 2.8 miles to end (Route 121). *Caution:* The end comes up suddenly at bottom of short hill.
- Left for 0.2 mile to Hancock Street on right.
- Right for 0.2 mile to diagonal crossroads (Burnt Swamp Road).
- Bear right for 1.3 miles to where Burnt Swamp Road turns left and main road curves right.
- Left for 0.8 mile to crossroads and stop sign (Torrey Road, un-marked).
- Straight for 0.9 mile to fork immediately after stop sign (Allen Street bears right).
- Bear left for 0.4 mile to fork where Fales Road bears right and High Street bears slightly left.

- Bear left for 0.7 mile to another fork where High Street turns left and main road bears right.
- Bear right for 1.4 miles to crossroads and stop sign (Route 120).
- Straight for 1.3 miles to end (Holmes Road on right, Sheldonville Road on left).
- Left for 1.1 miles to Cumberland Avenue (unmarked) on right. It's 0.3 mile after I–295 underpass.
- Right for 0.3 mile to first right (Cushman Road).
- Right for 0.2 mile to end.
- Left (still Cushman Road) for 1 mile to end (Mendon Road).
- Left for 0.2 mile to fork (May Street bears left).
- Bear left for 0.7 mile to traffic light (Route 1, Washington Street).
- Right for less than 0.2 mile to entrance to BJ's Wholesale Club on right.
- Turn right and just ahead bear left as you start to go uphill, passing behind the building of the shopping center from which you started.

18 miles

- Follow first 8 directions of long ride to Burnt Swamp Road on right.
- Right for 0.8 mile to crossroads and stop sign (Torrey Road, unmarked).
- Follow last 13 directions of long ride, beginning "Straight for 0.9 mile to fork . . ."

12 miles

- Follow first 4 directions of 28-mile ride, to Route 120.
- Right for 0.5 mile to crossroads, in Arnold Mills.
- Left for 0.2 mile to end (Route 120 again). You'll pass a small dam on your left.
- Right for 1.3 miles to Holmes Road (unmarked) on right. It immediately curves left parallel with the main road.
- Right for 1.6 miles to Cumberland Avenue (unmarked) on right. It's 0.3 mile after I–295 underpass.
- Follow last 7 directions of 28-mile ride.

Ray Young's Ride
Greenville–Chepachet–Mapleville

Number of miles:	20 (30 with Chepachet–Mapleville extension, 15 with shortcut)
Terrain:	Rolling, with several short, sharp hills.
Start:	NHD Hardware Store, in a small shopping center on Route 44, Greenville.
Food:	Grocery at corner of Snake Hill Road and Saw Mill Road, Glocester. Restaurant in Chepachet. Country store in Mapleville. Pizza at end.

This is a delightful ride along country lanes through the rolling and very rural landscape of the state's prime apple-growing region. The best time to bike here is in the first half of May, when apple blossoms cover the orchards in a delicate white canopy, or during harvest season in October and early November, when you can enjoy apples right off the tree.

The village of Greenville in the town of Smithfield is an attractive place to begin the ride. Notice the handsome stone church in the center of town. Within a mile you'll be in rolling orchard country, bobbing up and down small hills, none long enough to be discouraging. Peeptoad Road, across the town line in Scituate, is an appealing lane winding past an observatory belonging to the Skyscrapers, an amateur astronomy club. A pristine little pond lies at the end of the road.

As you swing west and then north, the landscape becomes more rural, with weathered barns and an occasional house tucked away in the woods. A couple of longer climbs, counterbalanced by fast descents, bring you to Glocester, a thoroughly rural town dotted with lakes, orchards, and small farms. The 20-mile route curves southward

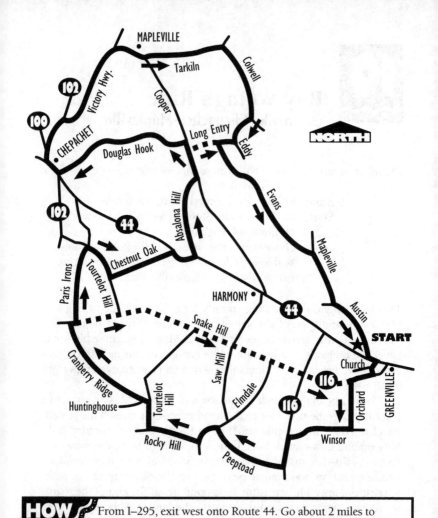

MAPLEVILLE

Tarkiln

Colwell

102

100

Victory Hwy.

Cooper

Long Entry

Eddy

NORTH

CHEPACHET

Douglas Hook

Evans

102

Absalona Hill

44

Chestnut Oak

Mapleville

Paris Irons

Tourtelot Hill

HARMONY

44

Austin

START

Snake Hill

Saw Mill

Church

Cranberry Ridge

Elmdale

116

Orchard

GREENVILLE

Huntinghouse

Tourtelot Hill

116

Winsor

Rocky Hill

Peeptoad

HOW
to get
there

From I–295, exit west onto Route 44. Go about 2 miles to hardware store on right, just past center of Greenville.

By bike from Providence, head west on Chalkstone Avenue. Cross bridge over small river into Johnston. Go 0.8 mile to second fork (Greenville Avenue bears left uphill). Bear left for 3 miles to where Greenville Avenue turns left downhill. Left for 1.4 miles to end (Route 44). Left for 0.2 mile to hardware store on right.

DIREC-TIONS

for the ride

30 miles

- Left on Route 44 for 100 yards to first right (Church Street), at blinking light. *Caution:* It's safest to walk this short stretch if traffic is heavy.
- Right for 0.1 mile to first left (still Church Street, unmarked).
- Left and just ahead right at end (Route 116, Smith Avenue). Go almost 0.5 mile to Orchard Avenue on left, almost at top of hill.
- Left for 0.8 mile to end (Winsor Avenue, unmarked).
- Right for 1 mile to end (Route 116).
- Left for 0.7 mile to Peeptoad Road, which turns sharply right.
- Make a sharp right for 1.4 miles to end.
- Left for 0.4 mile to Rocky Hill Road on right.
- Right for 1.1 miles to Tourtelot Hill Road on right
- Right for 0.7 mile to Huntinghouse Road on left.
- Left for 0.2 mile to fork (Cranberry Ridge Road bears right).
- Bear right for 1.4 miles to end (Snake Hill Road).
- Right for 0.2 mile to Paris Irons Road on left. The 15-mile ride goes straight here.
- Left for 1.1 miles to end.
- Right for 0.5 mile to Chestnut Oak Road on left.
- Left for 1.2 miles to end (Route 44). *Caution:* Steep, bumpy descent.
- Right for 0.5 mile to Absalona Hill Road on left.
- Left for 1.5 miles to end (Cooper Road, unmarked). *Caution* making left turn.
- Left for 0.5 mile to Long Entry Road on right, at bottom of hill. *Caution:* Gravelly spots. The 20-mile ride turns right here.
- Straight for 0.2 mile to Douglas Hook Road on left.
- Left for 2.7 miles to end (Route 44), in Chepachet.
- Right for 0.2 mile to fork, at blinking light (Routes 102 and 100 bear right).
- Bear right and just ahead bear right again on Route 102. Go 0.9 mile to unmarked road on right, midway up hill (Victory Highway, Old Route 102).

- Right for 1.7 miles to fork with garage in middle, in Mapleville.
- Bear right and just ahead bear right again at yield sign. Go 0.2 mile to Tarkiln Road, which bears left.
- Bear left for 2.2 miles to fork (Colwell Road bears right).
- Bear right for 0.8 mile to fork (entrance to golf course bears right, main road bears left).
- Bear left for 1 mile to Long Entry Road on right, immediately after main road curves sharply left.
- Right for 0.7 mile to end, at traffic island (Eddy Road on left).
- Right for 0.3 mile to Evans Road on left.
- Left for 3.7 miles to end (Austin Avenue), at T intersection.
- Left for 1.3 miles to end (Route 44).
- Turn right. Parking lot is just ahead on right.

20 miles

- Follow first 19 directions of 30-mile ride, to Long Entry Road.
- Right for 0.6 mile to fork (Evans Road bears right). *Caution:* Gravelly spots.
- Bear right for 3.7 miles to end (Austin Avenue), at T intersection.
- Left for 1.3 miles to end (Route 44).
- Turn right. Parking lot is just ahead on right.

15 miles

- Follow first 13 directions of 30-mile ride, to Paris Irons Road.
- Straight for 5.6 miles to Church Street on left, just before traffic light at Route 44.
- Left and just ahead right for 0.1 mile to end (Route 44).
- Left for 100 yards to parking lot on right. *Caution:* Route 44 is very busy; it's safest to walk this short stretch.

on Evans Road, another narrow byway that seems to have been designed with the bicyclist in mind. The last mile descends gradually back to Greenville.

The 30-mile ride heads farther northwest to Chepachet, the largest village in Glocester. It is attractive with lovely houses, many dating back to around 1800, and several antiques shops. The Brown & Hopkins Country Store has been in continuous operation since 1809. Next you'll go through Mapleville, a mill village at the edge of Burrillville, the most northwesterly town in the state. With a pair of grim-looking brick mills flanked by a row of identical dwellings originally built for the workers, Mapleville is typical of the many small mill villages that dot Rhode Island. A narrow back road takes you past a golf course to rejoin the short ride at Evans Road.

Chepachet–Scituate–Foster–East Killingly

Number of miles:	15 (31 with Foster–East Killingly extension)
Terrain:	Challenging; in other words, hilly.
Start:	CVS Pharmacy, corner of Route 44 and Douglas Hook Road, Chepachet. It's next to the post office.
Food:	No food on the short ride. Convenience store at junction of Routes 102 and 6 in Scituate. Country store at corner of Routes 94 and 101. Restaurant in Chepachet, at end.

This ride explores the wooded hills and unspoiled ponds of western Rhode Island, about 20 miles west of Providence. The terrain is hilly, but the effort expended in climbing will be rewarded by some exciting descents, including one of the longest in the state on the 31-mile ride. Because the region is thinly populated, you will not encounter much traffic. The only busy road, Route 101, has a safe and smooth shoulder.

From the ride's starting point in Chepachet, head south on Route 102, which climbs gradually through woodland to the top of Chopmist Hill, one of the highest points in the state, with an elevation of 730 feet. The short ride turns west on Route 101 and plunges down a spectacular descent with a sweeping view, only to climb again up Pray Hill, which you'll agree is appropriately named. Some maps spell it Prey, also appropriate. The return trip to Chepachet is nearly all downhill on rural lanes winding through dense forest and occasional patches of pasture. Shortly before the end is the Smith and Sayles Reservoir on Chestnut Hill Road.

The long ride continues south on Route 102 along the crest of Chopmist Hill. You'll pass the gracious Chopmist Hill Inn, known for its fine restaurant. Just ahead, revel in one of the state's longest downhills, a steady mile-long descent to the western edge of the Scituate Reservoir, the largest lake in Rhode Island. The picnic area at the bottom of the hill is a good spot for a breather; it has a pump where you can refill your water bottle with pure spring water if the handle hasn't been stolen. Just ahead, you can visit a lovely, isolated dam a half mile off the route.

A tough climb out of the watershed will bring you into the small village of Clayville. Now angle northwest through Foster, a completely rural town along the Connecticut border. In the tiny center of town, 100 yards to the left of Route 94 about 2 miles beyond Clayville, is the country's oldest town hall (built in 1796) that is still in use. A mile ahead, Rhode Island's only covered bridge (built in 1994) lies 100 yards off the route. Continue on to East Killingly Road, a rural byway that brings you to the Connecticut border, past the graceful North Foster Baptist Church and the Maple Glen Inn, an elegant restaurant.

A narrow road takes you into Connecticut, descending steeply into the mill village of East Killingly. Just before the village you'll parallel a chain of three small millponds, with two dams on your left. The second dam is across from the old brick and stone mill; you'll miss it unless you look for it. Route 101 takes you out of town and up a steep climb to the Rhode Island line. A more gradual ascent leads to the summit of Jerimoth Hill, the highest point in Rhode Island, with an elevation of 812 feet. Descend slowly for a half mile, passing the state's largest sawmill, and climb sharply once more to the top of Pray Hill to rejoin the short ride.

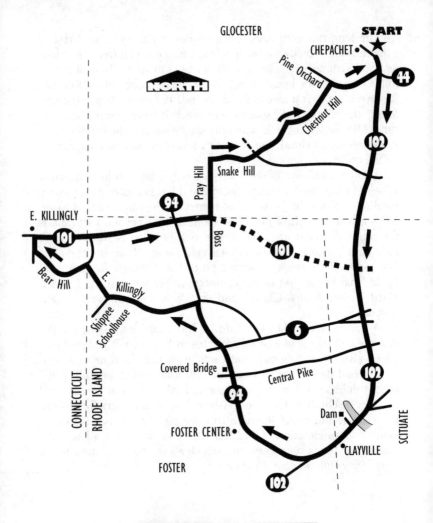

GLOCESTER

START

CHEPACHET

Pine Orchard

Chestnut Hill

44

NORTH

102

Snake Hill

Pray Hill

94

E. KILLINGLY

101

Boss

101

Bear Hill

E. Killingly

Shippee Schoolhouse

6

CONNECTICUT

RHODE ISLAND

Covered Bridge

Central Pike

102

94

Dam

FOSTER CENTER

SCITUATE

CLAYVILLE

FOSTER

102

HOW to get there — From I–295, exit west onto Route 44 and go about 9 miles to parking lot on right, at corner of Douglas Hook Road.

DIREC-TIONS
for the ride

31 miles

- Left on Route 44 for 0.3 mile to fork, at blinking light (Route 102 bears right).
- Bear slightly right for 4.6 miles to second traffic light (Route 101). Here the short ride turns right.
- Straight for 5.8 miles to fork where Routes 14 and 102 bear left and Route 94 bears right, about a mile beyond Clayville. (To visit dam, turn right after 3.9 miles onto Ponagansett Road, just past bottom of long, steady hill and a small bridge. Go 0.4 mile and turn left for 100 yards.)
- Bear right on Route 94 for 3.9 miles to Route 6, at stop sign and blinking light.
  To see covered bridge, turn left after 2.9 miles at crossroads onto dirt road (Central Pike, unmarked) for 100 yards.
- Straight for 1.3 miles to crossroads (East Killingly Road).
- Left for 1.6 miles to fork (Shippee Schoolhouse Road, unmarked, bears left).
- Bear right for 0.9 mile to another fork (Bear Hill Road, unmarked, bears left).
- Bear left for 1.7 miles to end (merge right at stop sign, in East Killingly). *Caution:* Steep, curving descent with sandy spots.
- Bear right for 0.1 mile to end (Route 101).
- Right for 4.3 miles to second crossroads and blinking light, at top of hill (Boss Road on right, Pray Hill Road on left).
- Left for 2.3 miles to fork immediately after stop sign (Snake Hill Road bears right, Chestnut Hill Road bears left).
- Bear left for 0.9 mile to a wide intersection where a smaller road goes straight and the main road curves left.
- Curve left for 2.1 miles to end (Pine Orchard Road on left, Chestnut Hill Road on right).
- Turn right and stay on main road for 1 mile to end (Route 44).
- Left for 0.3 mile to parking lot on right.

15 miles

- Follow first 2 directions of long ride, to Route 101.

- Right for 3.4 miles to blinking light at top of hill (Boss Road on left, Pray Hill Road on right).
- Right for 2.3 miles to fork immediately after stop sign (Snake Hill Road bears right, Chestnut Hill Road bears left).
- Follow last 3 directions of long ride.

Scituate Spins, 1 and 2

Number of miles: 16 (Scituate Spin 1) or 18 (Scituate Spin 2)
Terrain: Rolling, with one long hill on each ride.
Start: North Scituate Town Common, Route 116, just south of Route 6.
Food: Fruit and vegetable stand on Route 116. Grocery, corner of Snake Hill Road and Sawmill Road. Convenience store at junction of Routes 102 and 6. Snack bars in North Scituate, at end.

The town of Scituate, 10 to 15 miles west of Providence, provides superb bicycling on a network of winding, wooded roads with very little traffic. The town is dominated by the state's largest lake, the Scituate Reservoir. Here are a pair of rides that loop through the northern half of the town, leading you along back roads through boulder-strewn forests, across the reservoir's northern arm, and past several apple orchards. Although the two rides are in the same area, there is almost no overlap between them.

Both rides begin in North Scituate, the largest village in the town of Scituate. It is an attractive community of old homes, with a handsome brick library and a graceful white church opposite the Common. Behind the Common is an elegant white apartment building with tall columns that was formerly the Watchman Institute, an early school for African-American students. In early October, North Scituate comes alive as the site of Rhode Island's second largest art festival.

For the first ride, head south out of town on Route 116, riding through the dense evergreens banking the northern arm of the reservoir. Turn west on Route 14 and enjoy the long descent to the causeway that curves across the northern arm. Now you must tackle the

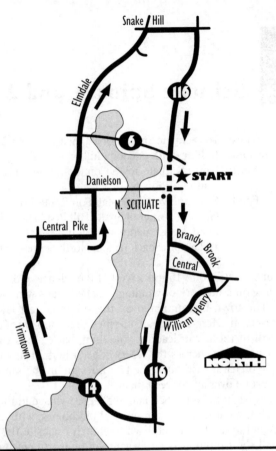

Snake Hill

Elmdale

116

6

Danielson

★ START

N. SCITUATE

Central Pike

Brandy Brook

Central

William Henry

Trimtown

116

14

NORTH

HOW to get there From I–295, exit west on Route 6 for about 3 miles to fork. Bear right (still Route 6) for 0.5 mile to Route 116. Turn left for 0.2 mile to parking lot on left, across from church.

By bike from Providence, head west from Olneyville Square on Plainfield Street. Go 0.8 mile to Killingly Street on right, opposite Lowell Avenue. Bear right for 0.3 mile to fork. Bear left uphill for 1.7 miles to traffic light (Route 5). Straight for 2.5 miles to fork (Bishop Road bears right). Bear right for 1.2 miles to fork (Pine Hill Road bears left). Bear left for 1.2 miles to end (Danielson Pike). Left for 0.2 mile to Route 116. Right for 0.2 mile to parking lot on right, opposite church.

Scituate Spin 1

■ Left on Route 116 for 0.2 mile to traffic light (Danielson Pike).
■ Straight for 0.6 mile to Brandy Brook Road.
■ Left for 0.9 mile to crossroads and stop sign (Central Avenue, unmarked). You'll climb gradually.
■ Straight for 0.1 mile to stop sign (merge left on William Henry Road). You will turn sharply right here.
■ Sharp right for 1.2 miles to end (Route 116).
■ Left for 1.5 miles to Route 14, at stop sign and blinking light.
■ Right for 2.1 miles to Trimtown Road on right, at top of hill.
■ Right for 2 miles to crossroads (Central Pike, unmarked).
■ Right for 1.5 miles to end (Danielson Pike, unmarked). *Caution:* Road curves 90 degrees left at bottom of big hill.
■ Left for 0.3 mile to Elmdale Road on right.
■ Right for 0.6 mile to crossroads and stop sign (Route 6).
■ Go straight. Stay on main road for 1.8 miles to where a wider road turns right and a smaller road bears slightly left.
■ Bear left (still Elmdale Road) for 0.6 mile to crossroads and stop sign (Snake Hill Road).
■ Right for 0.5 mile to crossroads and stop sign (Route 116 South on right).
■ Right for 1.9 miles to traffic light (Route 6).
■ Straight for 0.2 mile to parking lot on left.

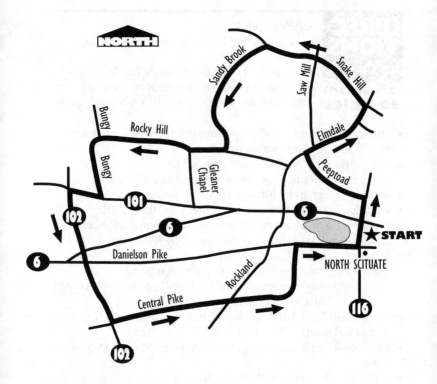

**DIREC-
TIONS**
for the ride

18 miles

Scituate Spin 2

- Right on Route 116 for 0.2 mile to traffic light (Route 6).
- Straight for 0.4 mile to Peeptoad Road on left.
- Left for 1.4 miles to end (Elmdale Road).
- Right for 0.7 mile to where a wider road turns right and a smaller road bears slightly left.
- Bear left (still Elmdale Road) for 0.5 mile to crossroads and stop sign (Snake Hill Road).

- Left for 1.1 miles to crossroads and blinking light (Saw Mill Road).
- Straight for 0.8 mile to Sandy Brook Road, which bears left downhill.
- Bear left for 2.2 miles to end (Rocky Hill Road, unmarked).
- Right for 0.7 mile to where Gleaner Chapel Road turns left and main road bears right.
- Bear right for 1.4 miles to where Bungy Road turns right and main road bears left. Climb steeply for 0.3 mile at beginning, then gradually for 1 mile.
- Bear left for 1 mile to end (Route 101).
- Right for 0.6 mile to traffic light (Route 102).
- Left for 1.1 miles to traffic light (Route 6). Just ahead is another light. Straight for 1.1 miles to crossroads (Central Pike, unmarked).
- Left for 1.8 miles to diagonal crossroads and stop sign at bottom of hill (Rockland Road, unmarked).
- Straight for 1.5 miles to end (Danielson Pike, unmarked). *Caution:* Road curves 90 degrees left at bottom of big hill.
- Right for 1 mile to traffic light (Route 116), in North Scituate.
- Left for 0.2 mile to parking lot on right.

---

toughest climb of the ride before heading north on Trimtown Road, which ascends gradually past homes nestled in the woods.

You'll be justly rewarded for the climb when you turn onto Central Pike, a smooth road that drops steeply back into the watershed. Opposite the end of the road is the headquarters of the State Police.

Just ahead turn onto Elmdale Road, an idyllic byway bobbing up and down small rises through dense, boulder-dotted woodland. You pass tiny Peeptoad Pond on your left and suddenly enter orchard country. The area north and west of here is the prime apple-growing region of Rhode Island, with orderly rows of apple trees covering the hillsides. Many of the orchards have fruit and cider stands that are good refreshment stops for a cyclist. Across the road, incongruous among the orchards, is an underground data storage area. Now turn south on Route 116 to finish the ride, passing a couple more orchards and Moswansicut Pond, set back from the road on the left.

The second ride heads northwest out of town on Peeptoad Road, a winding lane that seems to have been custom-designed for the bicyclist. You will pass the observatory of the Skyscrapers, an amateur astronomy club. Sandy Brook Road, another narrow country lane, snakes past two small ponds and a little dam. The one tough climb of the ride, on Rocky Hill Road, brings you onto Chopmist Hill, a long, high ridge. A fire tower and a pair of radio towers stand at the highest point. After a flat run along the ridge on Route 102, your reward comes on Central Pike, a smooth, lightly traveled road that runs primarily downhill for several miles past farms, weathered barns, and secluded country homes bordered by stone walls. Just before the end, pedal along the northern portion of the Scituate Reservoir.

Scituate–Foster

Number of miles:	19 (28 with Connecticut border extension)
Terrain:	Rolling, with two difficult climbs. To reward your efforts, however, finish with one of the best descents in the state.
Start:	Picnic area at junction of Route 102, Route 14, and Rockland Road, known as Crazy Corners, in Scituate.
Food:	None on short ride. Grocery store and small restaurant on Route 6.

Challenging but very scenic, this ride takes you through rural Rhode Island at its finest. Foster, an unspoiled country town hugging the Connecticut border 20 miles west of Providence, is a magnificent bicycling area of winding roller-coaster roads, passing small farms edged by stone walls, with old weathered barns.

The ride begins in Scituate at the western edge of the Scituate Reservoir. (A half mile from the start, just off the route, you can visit a beautiful dam along the small stream connecting the Barden and Scituate reservoirs.) You parallel the western arm of the reservoir on Route 12, a quiet, well-paved road. After a couple of miles turn west onto Old Plainfield Pike, which climbs gradually with an occasional steep pitch. Originally this road continued farther east across land that is now beneath the reservoir.

When the route turns north onto Howard Hill Road, there is a gentle downhill ride drifting past sturdy farmhouses, a tiny cemetery, and pastures dotted with cows and horses. You pass through Foster Center, whose Town House is the nation's oldest town hall in contin-

uous use (since 1822). Rhode Island's only covered bridge is 0.1 mile off the route as you turn east onto Central Pike to begin the most exciting portion of the ride. A screaming descent on the freshly repaved road zips you to the small bridge across the Barden Reservoir; then you pay the price on a sweat-producing grind up to Route 102. But once again you'll be rewarded with a long, steady downgrade back to your starting point, guaranteed to leave you in good spirits.

The long ride heads farther west, inching toward the Connecticut state line on more peaceful back roads. The terrain levels out for the remainder of the longer loop shortly before you turn north on Cucumber Hill Road. On Route 6, the only busy road on the ride, you can stop for a breather at a small restaurant or grocery store. After several more miles along narrow wooded roads, rejoin the short ride for the Central Pike portion of the ride.

FOSTER   SCITUATE

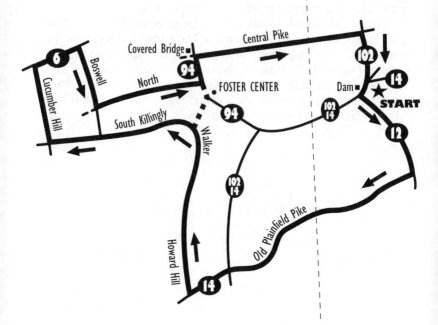

Central Pike

Covered Bridge
94

Boswell

North

Cucumber Hill

FOSTER CENTER

94

South Killingly

Walker

Dam

102
14

START

102
14

102
14

Old Plainfield Pike

Howard Hill

14

HOW to get there
From I–295, exit west on Route 14. Picnic area is 9 miles ahead on right.

DIREC-TIONS
for the ride

28 miles

(Before you leave, fill your water bottle from the pump between Route 102 and Rockland Road, if the handle hasn't been stolen.)

■ Head south (downhill) on Route 102 for 0.6 mile to Route 12 (Tunk Hill Road) on left. (To visit dam, turn right after 0.4 mile on Ponagansett Road for 0.4 mile and then go left for 100 yards.)

■ Left for 2.5 miles to Old Plainfield Pike on right, at top of hill.
■ Right for 4.3 miles to crossroads and stop sign (Route 102).
■ Straight onto Route 14 (unmarked) for 1.1 miles to Howard Hill Road on right.
■ Right for 3.8 miles to stop sign where South Killingly Road turns left and Walker Road bears right. Both roads are unmarked. Here the short ride bears right.
■ Left for 3.3 miles to crossroads and stop sign (Cucumber Hill Road).
■ Right for 1.6 miles to Route 6 (Danielson Pike), at stop sign.
■ Right for 1.1 miles to Boswell Trail on right, just after gas station on left.
■ Right for 1.7 miles to crossroads (North Road). Dirt road on right.
■ Left for 2.3 miles to end (Route 94). *Caution:* Bumpy spots.
■ Left for 0.8 mile to crossroads (Central Pike, unmarked). Dirt road on left. Here the ride turns right, but if you turn left for 0.1 mile you'll come to Rhode Island's only covered bridge. It was burned in 1993 by local teenagers shortly after it was constructed, and it was rebuilt in 1994.
■ Right for 3.6 miles to crossroads and stop sign at top of hill (Route 102).
■ Right for 1.3 miles to picnic area on left.

19 miles

■ Follow first five directions of long ride to Walker Road, which bears right at stop sign.
■ Bear right for 0.5 mile to another fork, in Foster Center (note old bell-towered schoolhouse, now a library, on right).

Here the ride bears left, but if you make a sharp right for 50 yards the Foster Town House will be on your left.

- Bear left for 100 yards to end (Route 94).
- Left for 1.1 miles to crossroads (Central Pike, unmarked). Dirt road on left. Here the ride turns right, but if you turn left for 0.1 mile you'll come to Rhode Island's only covered bridge. It was burned in 1993 by local teenagers shortly after it was constructed, and it was rebuilt in 1994.
- Follow last two directions of long ride.

Western Cranston–
Hope–Scituate

Number of miles:	18 (29 with Hope–Scituate extension, 14 with shortcut)
Terrain:	Rolling, with tough hills on Phenix Avenue and Hope Road. The long ride is hilly.
Start:	Western Hills Junior High School, Phenix Avenue, Cranston.
Food:	Grocery and snack bar in Hope (29-mile ride). Snack bar at corner of Routes 116 and 14. Restaurant at corner of Route 14 and Pippin Orchard Road. Farm stand and cider mill on Pippin Orchard Road.

This ride will come to many as a pleasant surprise. When you think of Cranston, you probably picture the congested neighborhoods and busy arteries just south of Providence. But the western third of the city, beyond I–295, is still rural, with large tracts of open land. Pedaling along Hope and Seven Mile Roads, you would think you were in Iowa rather than less than 10 miles from downtown Providence.

You start the ride by heading south on Phenix Avenue, a wide, smooth road. Soon you bear off onto less-traveled roads and ascend gradually through open farmland. If you stop and look back over your left shoulder, you will enjoy the fine views along Hope Road.

After a couple of miles, enjoy a fast, smooth descent to the valley of the Pawtuxet River. Parallel the river, passing several brick and stone mills from the turn of the century as you nick the northeast corner of Coventry. Then swing northward, back into farmland along Seven Mile Road, a delight for bicycling. As you ascend gradually onto a ridge, extensive views unfold to the west.

You'll pass an attractive white church, several small cemeteries,

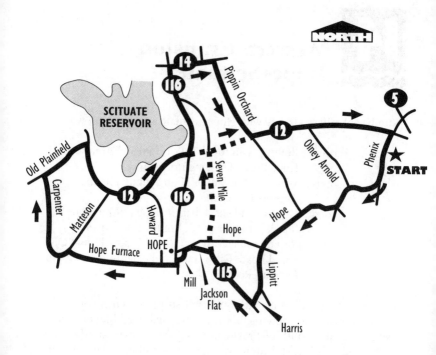

NORTH

SCITUATE
RESERVOIR

Old Plainfield

Carpenter

Matteson

12

Howard

HOPE

Hope Furnace

Mill

Jackson
Flat

115

Harris

Seven Mile

Hope

Lippitt

Hope

116

Pippin Orchard

14

116

12

Olney Arnold

Phenix

5

★
START

HOW
to get
there
From I–95 or I–295, exit onto Route 37 West and follow it to end (Natick Road). Right for 1.6 miles to school on right.

By bike from Providence, head southwest out of Olneyville Square on Pocasset Avenue. Go about 2 miles to Cranston Street, at traffic light. Right for 0.8 mile to Park Avenue, at traffic light. Right for 0.9 mile to school on left, shortly after second traffic light.

DIREC-TIONS
for the ride

29 miles

- Left on Phenix Avenue for 1.3 miles to where the main road curves left and a smaller road goes straight up a sharp hill.
- Straight uphill (still Phenix Avenue, unmarked) for 0.6 mile to fork (Olney Arnold Road bears right).
- Bear left for 0.4 mile to fork immediately after stop sign (Phenix Avenue bears left, Hope Road bears right).
- Bear right for 2.3 miles to crossroads and stop sign (Burlingame Road on left, Hope Road on right).
- Straight for 0.8 mile to Harris Street (unmarked), which bears right. The main road bears slightly left at the intersection.
- Bear right for 0.3 mile to end (Route 115). Mill village of Harris, which straddles the border of West Warwick and Coventry, is at end.
- Right for 0.9 mile to where Route 115 (Jackson Flat Road) turns left and Seven Mile Road (unmarked) goes straight. Here the short rides go straight.
- Left for 0.5 mile to blinking light (merge left).
- Bear left for 0.25 mile to Mill Street, which bears left just before end.
- Bear left for 0.2 mile to end (Route 116).
- Left for 0.1 mile to Hope Furnace Road on right.
- Right for 4 miles to end (Matteson Road, unmarked), at stop sign.
- Left for 0.25 mile to fork (Matteson Road bears left, Carpenter Road bears right).
- Bear right uphill for 2.2 miles to end (Old Plainfield Pike).
- Right for 1.3 miles to end (Route 12).
- Right for 3 miles to fork where the main road curves left and a smaller road (Howard Avenue, unmarked) goes straight.
- Curve left for 1.7 miles to stop sign and blinking light (Route 116).
- Left for 2 miles to Route 14, at blinking light.
- Right for 1.4 miles to Pippin Orchard Road on right.
- Right for 1.6 miles to crossroads and stop sign (Route 12, Scituate Avenue).

- Left for 3.2 miles to second traffic light (Phenix Avenue, unmarked). Route 12 turns left here.
- Right for 0.25 mile to school on left.

18 miles

- Follow first 7 directions of long ride, to Jackson Flat Road on left.
- Straight on Seven Mile Road (unmarked) for 2.2 miles to stop sign and blinking light (Route 12). Here the ride turns left, but to shorten the distance to 13.5 miles turn right. Go 4.3 miles to second traffic light (Route 12 turns left here), and right for 0.25 mile to school on left.
- Left for 1 mile to crossroads and stop sign (Route 116), at bottom of long, steep hill. *Caution* here.
- Right for 2 miles to blinking light (Route 14).
- Follow last 4 directions of long ride.

---

and the Curran Upper Reservoir before turning west onto Route 12. You will now enjoy a thrilling descent with a panoramic view of the Scituate Reservoir. The rest of the short ride continues along fine biking roads with good shoulders. From Route 116 watch for Betty Pond on your right. The last stretch along Route 12 is mostly downhill.

The long ride heads west to Hope, located in the southeastern corner of Scituate. You'll ride past a row of duplex mill houses facing each other across the street, with the four-story granite mill just ahead. Adjoining it is a brick addition, with a distinctive sawtooth roof designed to maximize the intake of natural light. A small canal diverts water from the Pawtuxet River to the mill.

As soon as you leave Hope, the landscape becomes densely forested, with an occasional house nestled in the woods off the narrow back roads. The area is typical of most of Scituate, an affluent town where one can live in relative privacy within a half-hour drive of Providence. After several miles you'll come to Route 12, a wonderful cycling road that follows the southern shore of the Scituate Reservoir. After two long climbs and descents, you'll cruise along the spectacular dam that holds the reservoir in place and rejoin the short ride just ahead.

Providence East-Side Ride

Number of miles: 10

Terrain: Rolling, with several short hills and one tough one.

Start: Eastside Marketplace, on Pitman Street opposite Butler Avenue, on the East Side of Providence.

Food: Several snack bars on Thayer Street, 2 blocks off the route near Brown University.

This is one of only two rides in the book that is urban rather than rural. Nine-tenths of Providence is unsuitable for enjoyable biking, but fortunately there is one section of the city, the East Side, that is tailor-made for a safe, leisurely two-wheel jaunt.

The East Side, situated between the downtown area and the Seekonk River, is the wealthiest and the most historic part of the city. The ride starts by following the river, which was formerly polluted but is now a clean and attractive waterway. You head inland briefly through a gracious residential area, passing Butler Hospital, a private psychiatric hospital that looks like an old graceful college campus.

Just north of the hospital is the rolling, meticulously landscaped Swan Point Cemetery, where little lanes, dipping up and down along the bluffs overlooking the river, wind past impressive crypts and monuments. This is where H. P. Lovecraft, America's best-known horror writer between Edgar Allan Poe and Stephen King, is interred.

Leaving the cemetery, head south on famed Blackstone Boulevard, the jogging capital of Rhode Island, with its broad, grassy center island and impressive homes on both sides. Then head across the middle of the East Side along Freeman Parkway, one of the finest streets in Providence, with its large, elegant residences. Just ahead is the

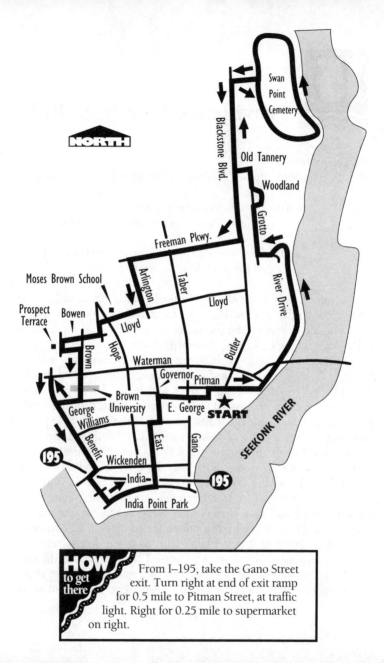

NORTH

Swan Point Cemetery

Blackstone Blvd.

Old Tannery

Woodland

Grotto

Freeman Pkwy.

Moses Brown School

Arlington

Taber

Lloyd

River Drive

Prospect Terrace

Bowen

Lloyd

Hope

Brown

Waterman

Butler

Governor

Pitman

Brown University

E. George

★ START

George Williams

Benefit

East

Gano

SEEKONK RIVER

195

Wickenden

India

195

India Point Park

HOW
to get there
From I–195, take the Gano Street exit. Turn right at end of exit ramp for 0.5 mile to Pitman Street, at traffic light. Right for 0.25 mile to supermarket on right.

- Right on Pitman Street for 0.25 mile to small rotary (Seekonk River on right). Pass Richmond Square, formerly an old factory, now a high-tech office park.
- Straight along river for 0.9 mile to end, at stop sign (merge right at top of steep hill on Loring Avenue).

- Bear right for 1 block to end (Grotto Avenue, unmarked).
- Right for 0.25 mile to Woodland Terrace on right, just before DO NOT ENTER sign.
- Right before 0.2 mile to end (Grotto Avenue again).
- Turn right and stay in same direction for 0.2 mile to end (Old Tannery Road).
- Left for 0.1 mile to end (Blackstone Boulevard).
- Right for 0.5 mile to entrance to Swan Point Cemetery on right.
- Bear right into the cemetery, explore it, and leave it at the same place you entered. (There is only one entrance.) Please ride slowly in the cemetery, which graciously allows bicycling. The privilege could be revoked if people ride carelessly.
- Bear left on Blackstone Boulevard for 0.9 mile to Freeman Parkway, after Upton Avenue and house number 180.
- Right for 0.6 mile to Arlington Avenue on left, just past steep part of hill.
- Left for 0.25 mile to crossroads and stop sign (Lloyd Avenue).
- Right for 0.3 mile to traffic light (Hope Street, unmarked). Moses Brown School is on right just before the light.
- Straight for 1 block to crossroads and stop sign (Thayer Street, unmarked).
- Left and first right on Bowen Street for 0.3 mile to end (Congdon Street). Brown University dormitories on left at beginning of Bowen Street.
- Left for 1 block to first left (Cushing Street, unmarked). Prospect Terrace is on right.
- Left for 0.2 mile to second crossroads (Brown Street, unmarked).
- Right for 0.2 mile to end (Waterman Street).
- Straight through arch into main quadrangle of Brown University.

Go 0.1 mile to first street (George Street). *Caution:* Curb at George Street.

- Right for 0.2 mile to end at Benefit Street (unmarked). *Caution:* Steep downhill.
- Right for 2 blocks to traffic light (Waterman Street). First Baptist Church is on left just past light. Here the ride makes a U-turn, but it's worth continuing 0.5 mile to the end to see the fine architecture on Benefit Street.
- Make a U-turn. Go south on Benefit Street for 0.6 mile to traffic light at bottom of hill (Wickenden Street).
- Right for 100 yards to another light, immediately after going under I–195.
- Left on South Main Street (unmarked). *Caution* turning left. Go 0.2 mile to end (India Street), where the waterfront is behind the building in front of you. You'll cross the hurricane barrier, a stone embankment with steel gates that can be slid shut across the road.
- Left for 0.3 mile to footbridge that crosses India Street and I–195. If you wish, you may ride on the footpaths along the water in India Point Park, which is just past a nightclub on right. Some sections of the footpath are gravel. A paved path continues 0.3 mile beyond the footbridge and loops around India Point, which forms the southeastern corner of Providence. *Caution:* Watch for pedestrians if you ride in the park.
- Cross the footbridge. *Caution:* The ramp has tight U-turns; it's safer to walk. At far end of footbridge go straight onto East Street (unmarked), passing Tockwotton Home, a residence for the elderly, on left. Go 0.25 mile to end (Williams Street).
- Right for 1 block to crossroads and stop sign (Governor Street).
- Left for 0.2 mile to third right (East George Street).
- Turn right. After 3 blocks the street turns left at stop sign. Continue 1 block to crossroads and stop sign (Pitman Street, unmarked). *Caution* at second crossroads (Gano Street); it is very busy.
- Right for 0.1 mile to supermarket on right.

Moses Brown School, an exclusive prep school with a magnificent old campus. Now cross Thayer Street, the main commercial "strip" for the Brown University community. Here are three blocks lined with boutiques, bookstores, little restaurants, and the enduring Avon movie theater. An unlocked bike here has a life expectancy of about one minute.

You now climb gradually to the crest of College Hill, which drops steeply toward the downtown area. Perched on the brow of the hill is Prospect Terrace, a grassy overlook with a superb view of the city. On the grounds is a large statue of Roger Williams, who is interred here.

A few blocks ahead, cross the central quadrangle of Brown University, containing its oldest building, University Hall, built in 1770. A block from the campus is historic Benefit Street, which runs along the side of College Hill one block up from the downtown area. In quick succession, you pass an impressive cluster of historic landmarks, beginning with the flawlessly preserved First Baptist Church, built in 1775, and the Museum of Art of the Rhode Island School of Design, one of the country's finest small museums. Across the street is the Providence Athenaeum, a private library open to visitors, built in 1838 in Greek Revival style. Next is the imposing, brick Superior Courthouse, opposite Athenaeum Row, a graceful brick apartment house built in 1856. Immediately beyond the courthouse is the Stephen Hopkins House (1707 with 1743 addition), home of the ten-time governor of Rhode Island and signer of the Declaration of Independence.

Continuing south on Benefit Street, pass the graceful First Unitarian Church (1816), which contains the largest bell cast by Paul Revere, and the palatial John Brown House (1786), which John Quincy Adams described as "the most magnificent and elegant private mansion that I have ever seen on this continent." After amassing a fortune as a China trade merchant, slave trader, and privateer, John Brown wanted to build a mansion that would awe and inspire his visitors. It is now owned by the Rhode Island Historical Society and is open to the public.

Just past the foot of Benefit Street, you go along the southern edge of the East Side, fronting on Providence Harbor. This is an area where old warehouses and factories have been replaced by, or recycled into, nightclubs and luxury condominiums. Cross the Fox Point Hurricane Barrier, a series of gates that can be closed to prevent storm-driven water from flooding the city as it did during the terrible hurricanes of 1938 and 1954. Just ahead is the dock for the ferry to Newport and Block Island, a superb four-hour trip. The rest of the waterfront consists of India Point Park.

The last mile of the ride goes through a predominantly Portuguese neighborhood of well-kept, closely spaced dwellings.

Coventry–West Greenwich

Number of miles: 16 (28 with West Greenwich extension)
Terrain: Rolling, with some long, steady hills. The long ride is hilly, with two real monsters.
Start: Coventry Plaza, Route 3, Coventry.
Food: Genuine, old-fashioned country store in Summit. Burger King at end and McDonald's across the road.

This ride is a tour of the sparsely populated countryside that extends west toward the Connecticut border from the center of the state. It begins in Coventry, a long, rectangular town that extends from the Connecticut state line east to just 5 miles from Narragansett Bay. This is a town with two sharply contrasting sections. The eastern third is fairly built up, but the western section is completely rural, with only the three tiny villages of Coventry Center, Summit, and Greene tucked away amidst the rocky, wooded landscape.

The starting point lies on the dividing line between these two sections. After a brief stretch on Route 3, you head into woodland when you turn onto Hill Farm Road. Cross a small bridge over the Flat River Reservoir that feeds into the Pawtuxet River. The road climbs gradually onto a forested ridge that drops down to the reservoir on your right. Cross Route 117 in Coventry Center, a small village with a couple of old mills, then ride alongside the Flat River Reservoir (also called Johnsons Pond), and rejoin Route 117, a wide, well-paved road with a good shoulder and not much traffic.

You proceed to the village of Summit, containing a few old houses, small church, and marvelous old-fashioned country store hidden on a back road, which used to be part of Route 117. The short ride turns south briefly past rich farmland and a little pond and then

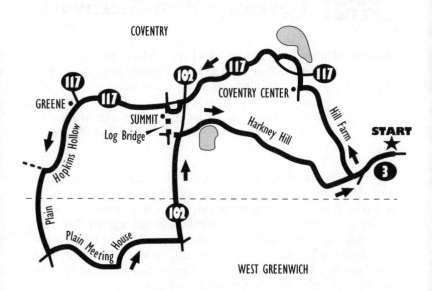

NORTH

COVENTRY

117

GREENE •

117

102

117

117

COVENTRY CENTER •

SUMMIT •

Log Bridge

Harkney Hill

Hill Farm

START

★

3

Hopkins Hollow

Plain

102

Plain Meeting House

WEST GREENWICH

HOW to get there From I–95, exit north onto Route 3 at exit 6. Go 2 miles to shopping center on left, at traffic light.

DIREC-TIONS

for the ride

28 miles

- Right out of parking lot for 1.1 miles to Harkney Hill Road, at fourth traffic light.
- Right for 0.2 mile to Hill Farm Road on right.
- Right for 3.1 miles to crossroads and stop sign (Route 117).
- Straight for 0.7 mile to end (Route 117 again).
- Right for 3.1 miles to crossroads and stop sign (Route 102).
- Straight and then immediately left on Old Summit Road. Go 0.3 mile to end (Log Bridge Road). Country store on corner. Here the short ride turns left.
- Right for 0.1 mile to crossroads and stop sign (Route 117).
- Left for 2.6 miles to stop sign where Route 117 turns right, in Greene.
- Go straight onto Hopkins Hollow Road. After 2.2 miles, main road curves sharply left up steep hill. Continue 2.1 miles to crossroads and stop sign (Liberty Hill Road on right, Plain Meeting House Road on left).
- Left for 3.7 miles to crossroads and stop sign (Route 102).
- Left for 2.6 miles to crossroads and blinking light at top of hill (Route 118, Harkney Hill Road on right).
- Right for 5.4 miles to end (Route 3).
- Left for 1.1 miles to shopping center on left, at fourth traffic light.

16 miles

- Follow first 6 directions of long ride, to end of Old Summit Road.
- Left for 0.7 mile to crossroads.
- Left for 0.1 mile to blinking light (Route 102).
- Straight on Harkney Hill Road (unmarked) for 5.4 miles to end (Route 3).
- Left for 1.1 miles to shopping center on left, at fourth traffic light.

begins the return leg on Harkney Hill Road. You pass the Quidneck Reservoir, surrounded by forests and some cabins belonging to summer camps. The road winds through deep woods for 2 miles and then plunges down the greatest descent of the ride. As you begin to go downhill, enjoy the sweeping view of the countryside. Just beyond the bottom of the hill, cross two narrow inlets of the Flat River Reservoir and rejoin Route 3 a mile from the starting point.

The long ride heads farther west along Route 117, now a narrow secondary road, to the picturesque village of Greene, only 2 miles from the Connecticut line. Here you turn south on a rustic lane that twists past rambling old farmhouses and untouched Tillinghast Pond. You must tackle a short but very steep hill that greets you just as you go around a sharp curve. Continue into West Greenwich with its small, simple church dating from 1750. Turn east on Plain Meeting House Road for the most challenging section of the ride. You drop quickly into a hollow but then fight your way out up one of the longest hills in Rhode Island, ascending 350 feet in nearly a mile. At the summit you can breathe a sigh of relief, because the rest of the ride is easy, except for one more steep hill about a quarter mile long. You rejoin the short ride about 3 miles before the glorious descent back to Route 3.

East Greenwich–North Kingstown–Goddard Memorial State Park

Number of miles:	16 (25 with North Kingstown extension)
Terrain:	Rolling, with several short, steep hills.
Start:	Greenwich Village Shopping Center, Route 1, East Greenwich, 0.4 mile south of Route 401.
Food:	Convenience store on Route 2 at Middle Road. Convenience store and pizza on Route 2 at Frenchtown Road. Convenience store on Route 2 near South Road (long ride). Burger King, Route 1 at Newcomb Road, North Kingstown (long ride). Cafe at end.
Facilities:	Rest rooms at Goddard Memorial State Park.

Just south of Warwick, as the Providence metropolitan area begins to thin out, pleasant bicycling abounds on smooth, lightly traveled roads winding through the rocky, wooded landscape. The short ride explores East Greenwich, which boasts the highest per-capita income of the Rhode Island towns. The center of town, along Route 1, retains the ambience of a turn-of-the-century community with its brick commercial buildings. Of historic interest are the former Kent County Courthouse, built in 1750 and enlarged in 1805; and the fortresslike Varnum Memorial Armory, containing a military museum. Old homes, many built over a century ago, perch on the steep hillside between Route 1 and the bay. West of town, most of the newer homes lie on large wooded lots, well integrated with the landscape, giving a rustic rather than a suburban flavor to the area.

Begin the ride by heading along the waterfront on Greenwich Cove, a small inlet of Greenwich Bay, which is in turn an inlet of Nar-

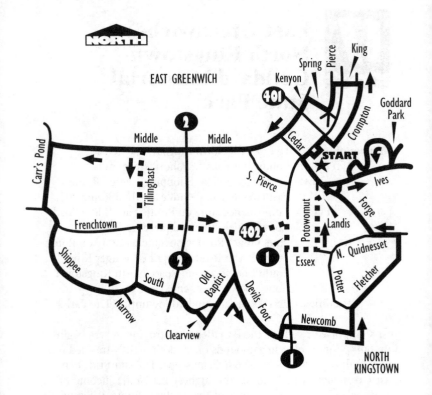

NORTH

EAST GREENWICH

King
Spring
Pierce
Kenyon
401
Goddard Park
Crompton
Middle
Middle
Cedar
START
Carr's Pond
2
S. Pierce
Ives
Tillinghast
Forge
Frenchtown
Potowomut
Landis
402
N. Quidnesset
Shippee
2
1
Essex
South
Old Baptist
Devils Foot
Potter
Fletcher
Narrow
Clearview
Newcomb
1
NORTH KINGSTOWN

HOW to get there
From the north, head south on I–95 to Route 4, bear left, and just ahead take the Route 401 exit. Turn right (east) at end of ramp and go 2.5 miles to traffic light (Route 1). Turn right, and shopping center is 0.4 mile ahead on left.

From the south, exit south from I–95 onto Route 2 and immediately turn left on Route 401. Go 2.5 miles to traffic light (Route 1). Turn right, and shopping center is 0.4 mile ahead on left.

- Right on Route 1 and immediately right on Greenwich Boulevard, after cannons. Go 0.25 mile to end (Route 1 again).
  You may wish to walk up the short, steep hill at the beginning of Greenwich Boulevard.
- Right for 100 yards to first right, Upland Avenue (unmarked), just before Dunkin' Donuts.
- Right for 0.1 mile to end (Rocky Hollow Road, unmarked).
- Right for 0.1 mile to end (Crompton Avenue).
- Left at end. After 0.7 mile, road turns 90 degrees left on King Street at stop sign.
- Jog left and immediately right along water, go 0.1 mile to dead end, and backtrack to King Street.
- Right for 0.2 mile to Route 1, at second stop sign. Former Kent County Courthouse on far left corner.
- Straight for 100 yards to stairs and carry bike up them. The elegant James Mitchell Varnum House, built in 1773 is in front of you at top of stairs.
- Left at top of stairs for 0.2 mile to Spring Street, at third stop sign.
- Turn 90 degrees right for 0.5 mile to end (Kenyon Avenue).
- Left for less than 0.2 mile to traffic light (Route 401, First Avenue).
- Straight for 2.3 miles to traffic light (Route 2).
- Straight for 1 mile to Tillinghast Road on left. Here the short ride turns left.
- Curve right on Middle Road for 1.7 miles to end (Carr's Pond Road, unmarked).
- Turn left. Stay on main road for 1.8 miles to Shippee Road on right, at stop sign.
- Right for 1.8 miles to where Narrow Lane turns right and main road curves left.
- Curve left for 0.6 mile to stop sign (Tillinghast Road bears left, South Road turns right).
- Right for 0.9 mile to traffic light (Route 2).
- Straight for 0.5 mile to fork just after top of hill (Clearview Drive bears right).

- Bear right for 0.3 mile to end (Old Baptist Road, unmarked).
- Left for 1.3 miles to end (Devils Foot Road, Route 403).
- Right across railroad overpass for 1.3 miles to Namcook Road on left (sign says TO WICKFORD).
- Sharp left for 0.1 mile to Newcomb Road (unmarked) on right. A sign again says TO WICKFORD. (Burger King on right just before Newcomb Road. Enter and leave by back entrance.)
- Turn right and immediately cross Route 1 (Post Road) at traffic light. Go 1.7 miles to stop sign where Potter Road turns left and Fletcher Road bears right.
- Bear right for 1.7 miles to end (North Quidnesset Road, unmarked).
- Left for 0.4 mile to third right, Forge Road.
- Right for 1.1 miles to unmarked road on right, just before restaurant.
- Right for 100 yards to end (Ives Road, unmarked).
- Right for 1.4 miles to Goddard Park entrance on left.
- Left into park for 0.3 mile to fork. There is currently no entrance fee for bicyclists. At the fork the ride bears left, but if you bear right for 0.3 mile you come to the beach.
- Bear left for 1.5 miles to end (park exit). You may have to walk your bike around two barriers across the road during the colder half of the year.
- Right for 1 mile to shopping center on right, at Route 1.

16 miles

- Follow first 13 directions of long ride, to Tillinghast Road on left.
- Left for 1.3 miles to crossroads and stop sign (Frenchtown Road). Here the ride turns left, but if you turn right for 100 yards the Museum of Wireless and Steam will be on your left.
- Left for 1 mile to traffic light (Route 2, South County Trail).
- Straight for 1.4 miles to end (Route 1), at large traffic island.
- Right for 0.5 mile to Essex Road on left (traffic light). *Caution:* Walk across railroad overpass, where there is no shoulder, if traffic is heavy.

- Left (*Caution* here; it's safest to walk across) for 0.4 mile to Poto-womut Road on left.
- Left for 1 mile to Landis Drive on right. Notice dam on left after 0.2 mile, set back 50 yards from road.
- Right for 0.25 mile to end (Old Forge Road).
- Right for 50 yards, and then left for 100 yards to end (Ives Road, unmarked).
- Follow last 4 directions of long ride.

---

ragansett Bay. The slender, sheltered cove is an ideal spot to moor small boats. You bike past several marinas and some old waterfront buildings recycled into cozy restaurants and taverns. Then head inland, climbing a short, steep hill up to Route 1.

As you head west on Middle Road, the landscape becomes more and more suburban; after you cross Route 2 it becomes rural. The short ride turns south on Tillinghast Road, a delightful byway that rolls up and over small hills. The unique New England Museum of Wireless and Steam, open by appointment (401–884–1710), is 100 yards off the route. Two miles ahead you pass Browne and Sharpe Manufacturing Company, makers of machine tools and hydraulic equipment. During the early 1980s, the firm was on strike for nearly two years—one of the longest strikes in American labor history.

Proceed into the Potowomut section of Warwick, a peninsula protruding into Narragansett Bay. Goddard Memorial State Park, which lies along the northern shore, fronts on both Greenwich Cove and Greenwich Bay. A recreational showpiece and a pleasure for biking, the park was originally two country estates and contains nearly 500 acres of lawns, stately forest, and beach. On the grounds are a golf course, riding academy, and miles of bridle paths. When you leave the park, you're only a mile from the start.

The long ride first follows the ups and downs of Middle Road westward until its end; then a well-earned descent on Carr's Pond Road will reward your efforts. More downhills await you most of the way to Route 2. The stretch between Routes 2 and 1 is more suburban. After crossing Route 1, parallel North Kingstown's former Quonset Point Naval Air Station, where that hallmark of military architecture, the Quonset Hut, originated. At present, Quonset Point is an industrial park owned by the state and open to the public. On the former base, miles of roads pass by gigantic runways, docks, grim military buildings, and Electric Boat's submarine plant. A fascinating spot here is the Quonset Air Museum, which collects and restores military aircraft in an old brick hangar.

North of Quonset Point, you pedal through an area of gracious country estates and gentleman farms. After a relaxing descent to the Hunt River, rejoin the short ride for the circuit of Goddard Memorial State Park and return to the starting point.

The Connecticut Border
Voluntown–Sterling–Oneco–Escoheag

Number of miles: 31 (33 on optional route to Step Stone Falls and
Escoheag)
Terrain: Hilly.
Road surface: 2.7 miles of dirt road on the optional route to
Step Stone Falls and Escoheag (mountain bike
recommended).
Start: Beach Pond parking lot, Route 165, Exeter, just
before Connecticut border. There is a parking
fee on beach days.
Food: Pizza at Plainfield–Sterling line. Country store in
Oneco. Grocery and restaurant in Voluntown.
Snack bar at Stepping Stone Ranch, Escoheag.

The western edge of the state along the Connecticut border comes as
close to true wilderness as you'll find in Rhode Island. The paved-
road ride hugs the Connecticut side of the state line, climbing onto
ridges with spectacular views and plunging into small valleys. The
optional longer ride, which includes 2.7 miles along dirt roads, straddles the border, passing remote Bailey Pond and then Step Stone
Falls, a little-known beauty spot where a stream cascades over a succession of broad, steplike rocks.

   The ride starts from Beach Pond, a good-sized pond straddling the
state line. You immediately cross into Voluntown, Connecticut, a small
village surrounded by miles of woods and farmland. Its main claim to
fame is that for some reason the Committee for Nonviolent Action,
one of the first organizations opposed to the Vietnam War, was located
here. You wind up and down on narrow roads passing small farms and
then head north on Route 49, a paradise for bicycling. There's a very
gradual climb onto Ekonk Hill, a high open ridge where hundreds of

cows graze contentedly. From both sides of the road, superb views sweep to the horizon. You are now in Sterling, a slender town midway between the northeast and southeast corners of Connecticut.

Route 49 brings you into the tiny village of Sterling Hill, which has a lovely white church. The hamlet has been designated a National Historic District. Drop off the ridge in a screaming descent that keeps getting steeper and steeper. In the valley lies the mill village of Almyville, where a lovely terraced dam on the Moosup River stands between two abandoned mills.

From Almyville, it's a couple of miles to the center of Sterling, a small mill town with a row of identical houses facing the millpond. In a triumph of folk art, someone has painted a waving American flag on a large rock on the shore of the pond. Sterling is the site of a controversial new tire-burning plant, one of the largest in the world. You can see it on top of a hill as you come into town. Two miles beyond Sterling is Oneco, another attractive village (part of the township of Sterling) with a fine white church and an old-time country store built in 1879. From here, narrow lanes roll up and down past horse farms to the outskirts of Voluntown, where there's a restaurant about 4 miles from the end of the ride.

The dirt road option begins about 4 miles south of Oneco. Step Stone Falls (sometimes called Stepping Stone Falls) lies along the unpaved section about 4 miles after you cross into Rhode Island. Beyond the falls, the road twists up a very steep, rutted hill, which you'll want to walk. At the top is a paved road that goes through the village of Escoheag. This community boasts a fire tower, a few houses, two tiny cemeteries, an equally tiny church, and the town hot spot, the Stepping Stone Ranch. This sprawling establishment is primarily a place to board and ride horses, with innumerable trails webbing through the surrounding state forest lands. On summer weekends, the enterprising owner hosts special events like the popular Cajun Festival on Labor Day weekend (it is the largest outside of Louisiana).

Just past the ranch cross the town line into Exeter and enjoy the descent to Route 165. From here it's 2 miles back to Beach Pond and a well-earned swim.

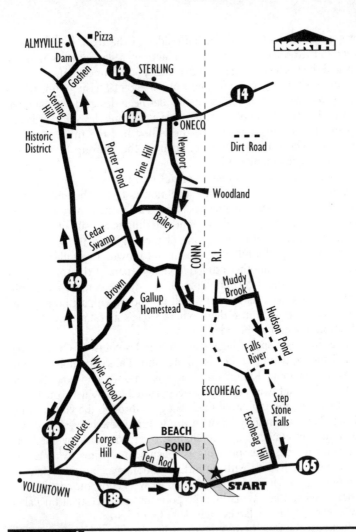

HOW to get there From the north, head south on I–95 to exit 6 (Route 3). Turn left (south) at end of ramp for about 6 miles to Route 165 on right. Turn right for about 8 miles to Beach Pond.

From the south, head north on I–95 to exit 4 (Route 3). Go north on Route 3 for about 3.5 miles to Route 165 on left. Turn left for about 8 miles to Beach Pond.

- Right on Route 165 for 1.3 miles to Bennett Road on right, almost at top of gradual hill.
- Jog right and immediately left on Ten Rod Road for 0.5 mile to end (merge left at stop sign).
- Sharp right on Forge Hill Road for 0.3 mile to Wylie School Road on left, at bottom of hill.
- Left for 2.6 miles to second crossroads and stop sign (Route 49). Notice former one-room schoolhouse, built in 1850, on far right corner.
- Right for 5.7 miles to end (Route 14A).
- Right for 0.2 mile to first left (Sterling Hill Road, unmarked).
- Left for 1.5 miles to Goshen Road (first right). It comes up suddenly while you're descending a short hill.
  The square building visible in the distance on your right near the beginning is the tire-burning plant.
- Right for 0.8 mile to unmarked road (first left).
- Left for 0.1 mile to blocked-off bridge; notice dam on right. Backtrack to main road.
- Left for 0.3 mile to end (Route 14). Here the ride turns right, but for pizza, turn left on Route 14 for 0.1 mile.
- Right on Route 14 (left if you're coming from the pizza shop) for 3 miles to unmarked road that bears right (sign says ONECO).
  You'll go through the center of Sterling after 1.9 miles. When you get to the road that bears right, a circular stone enclosure (the remains of a dog pound) is on the far side of the intersection.
- Bear right for 0.7 mile to end (Route 14A), in Oneco.
- Right for 0.25 mile to second left (Newport Road). Country store on corner.
- Left for 1.2 miles to fork (Woodland Road bears right).
- Bear right for 0.8 mile to end (Bailey Road, unmarked).
- Right for 0.9 mile to stop sign (merge left on Pine Hill Road).
- Bear left and just ahead curve left on main road. Go 0.2 mile to stop sign (merge left on Porter Pond Road).
- Bear left for 1.3 miles to second right (Brown Road), just after small pond on right. Here the dirt-road option goes straight.

- Right for 3.1 miles to end (Route 49). Steep 0.5 mile climb at beginning.
- Left for 2.5 miles to end (Route 138 and 165). Here the ride turns left, but if you turn right a grocery and pizza shop are just ahead on your left.
- Left (right if you're coming from the pizza shop) for 1.1 miles to fork where Route 138 bears right and Route 165 bears left.
- Bear left for 2.6 miles to parking lot on left.

Dirt-Road Option (33 miles)

- Follow the main ride to the junction of Porter Pond Road and Brown Road, 4.4 miles after the country store in Oneco.
- Straight on Gallup Homestead Road for 1.1 miles to end (Bailey Road, unmarked).
- Right for 1.8 miles to end (Hazard Road on left). The last 0.3 mile, after you cross into Rhode Island, is dirt. Bailey Pond is on your left just before the state line.
- Left on paved road for 0.1 mile to Muddy Brook Road on right.
- Right for 0.9 mile to end (Seth Brown Road on left, Hudson Pond Road on right).
- Turn right. After 0.7 mile the road becomes dirt. Continue 1.1 miles to where the main road curves 90 degrees right onto Falls River Road (unmarked).
- Curve right, and stay on dirt road for 0.5 mile to Step Stone Falls on left, at small bridge.
- Continue 0.6 mile up steep hill to end (Escoheag Hill Road, unmarked). Do yourself a favor and walk the bumpy and rocky hill.
- Left for 2.3 miles to crossroads and stop sign (Route 165).
- Right for 1.6 miles to parking lot on right.

That Dam Ride
Wyoming–Exeter–Rockville–Woodville

Number of miles:	17 (26 with Rockville–Woodville extension)
Terrain:	Rolling with two tough hills.
Start:	Vacant shopping center on the north side of Route 138, Wyoming, just west of I–95.
Food:	No food stops on the route. Several snack bars and a Chinese restaurant on Route 138 at end.
Facilities:	Rest rooms at gas station next to start.

This is an original ride of the Narragansett Bay Wheelmen and one of my personal favorites. It explores a very rural, wooded part of South County along the Connecticut border, going past tumbling brooks, millponds, and several fine dams. A long section of the ride runs through the wooded Arcadia Management Area, the largest expanse of state-owned land in Rhode Island.

Begin the ride in Wyoming and within a half mile pass the first dam, which is on the Wood River. Behind the dam is Wyoming Pond. Just ahead turn north on Old Nooseneck Hill Road, a good secondary road with almost no traffic. Follow the swift-moving river and cross it again; there's a lovely dam on your left. A mile farther, the main road turns right. Just beyond this point, if you go straight instead of right, there's a state fish hatchery (open 9:00 A.M. to 3:00 P.M., Monday through Friday). If you'd like to venture off the route, continue straight for 0.25 mile to the Tomaquag Indian Museum. In addition to showing exhibits, the museum also serves as a cultural center for the Narragansett Indian community, with a trading post and classes in Native-American crafts and history. Next to the museum is the Dovecrest, a restaurant run by Native Americans.

Back on the main road, you enter the Arcadia Management Area,

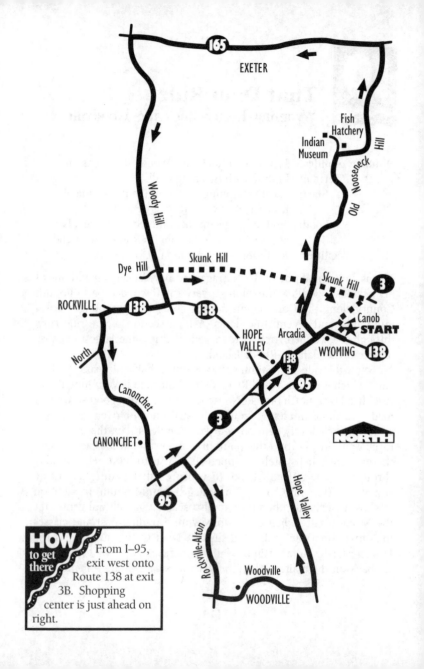

165

EXETER

Fish Hatchery

Indian Museum

Old Nooseneck Hill

Woody Hill

Dye Hill   Skunk Hill   Skunk Hill   3

ROCKVILLE   138   138   Canob   START

North   HOPE VALLEY   Arcadia   WYOMING   138

Canonchet   138 3

                                            3   95

CANONCHET

NORTH

95   Hope Valley

Rockville-Alton

95

                            Woodville
                            WOODVILLE

HOW to get there   From I-95, exit west onto Route 138 at exit 3B. Shopping center is just ahead on right.

- Right on Route 138 for 0.2 mile to traffic light (Route 3).
- Bear left and just ahead turn right on Arcadia Road. Stay on main road for 3.1 miles to where main road curves 90 degrees right uphill and a smaller road goes straight.

  Here the ride curves right, but go straight to see fish hatchery and Indian museum.
- Right for 2.4 miles to end (Route 165).
- Left for 3.9 miles to crossroads (Escoheag Hill Road on right, Woody Hill Road on left).
- Left for 3.5 miles to crossroads and stop sign (Dye Hill Road). *Caution:* Watch for bumps, potholes, and sandy spots for the first 2 miles. The short ride turns left at the crossroads.
- Straight for 0.6 mile to crossroads and stop sign (Route 138, Spring Street).
- Right for 0.9 mile to fork where Winchek Pond Road (unmarked) bears left into Rockville.
- Bear left and just ahead bear left again on Canonchet Road. Go 0.4 mile to fork.
- Bear left (still Canonchet Road, unmarked) for 1.8 miles to stop sign (Stubtown Road on right).
- Bear slightly left for 1.1 miles to crossroads and stop sign (Route 3).
- Left for 0.5 mile to divided road on right (sign says TO I–95).
- Right for 2.3 miles to crossroads and stop sign (Woodville Road). *Caution:* Bumpy sections.
- Left for 1.4 miles to end (Hope Valley Road, unmarked).
- Left for 3.3 miles to stop sign at top of hill.
- Bear right on main road for 0.2 mile to end (merge right on Route 3), in Hope Valley.
- Bear right for 0.9 mile to traffic light where Route 138 bears right.
- Bear right for 0.2 mile to parking lot on left.

17 miles

- Follow first 5 directions of long ride, to crossroads and stop sign (Dye Hill Road on right, Skunk Hill Road on left).

- Left for 2.7 miles to crossroads and stop sign (Old Nooseneck Hill Road, unmarked).
- Straight for 0.7 mile to diagonal crossroads and stop sign (Route 3).
- Sharp right for 0.6 mile to Canob Lane, which turns sharply left.
- Turn sharply left, and just ahead take the first right. Go less than 0.2 mile to gas station on left just before end.
- Left through gas station to parking lot of shopping center.

---

an extensive woodland area crisscrossed by hiking trails. You'll enjoy Browning Mill Pond, with its small beach and lovely brook that cascades under the road into the pond. Turn west onto Route 165, which runs through the Management Area for several miles. A steep, half-mile-long hill is followed by a descent of equal magnitude. The route turns south onto Woody Hill Road, a narrow lane twisting through evergreen forests and a few small farms. There's a steep but much shorter hill followed by a lazy descent. Finish the short ride by heading east on Skunk Hill Road past pleasant patches of open farmland and the northern end of Wyoming Pond.

The long ride proceeds farther south to Route 138, where you pedal by two small ponds and the handsome red-brick Centerville mill. Just ahead, turn onto a back road through Rockville, a tiny village with a short row of frame houses with peaked roofs, and an old stone mill. The ride continues south on Canonchet Road, a wooded lane that leads mostly downhill to Route 3. You pass undeveloped Ashville Pond and go through Canonchet, another miniscule village with a few old homes and a small stone mill that is now a plastics factory. Soon you coast downhill into Woodville, the most attractive of the mill villages on the ride, with three gracious wooden homes overlooking another fine dam on the Wood River. As you descend into the village, slow down to appreciate this picturesque spot.

The last stretch to Wyoming goes along a smooth, mostly flat road. Just before town there's a brick mill built in 1869 with yet another dam beside it. You pass the Hack and Livery General Store, a crafts and gift shop with a big selection of penny candy.

Richmond–Exeter–
Carolina–Shannock

Number of miles:	18 (30 with Carolina–Shannock extension)
Terrain:	Rolling, with two long hills and several shorter ones.
Start:	Vacant shopping center on the north side of Route 138, Wyoming, just west of I–95.
Food:	Snack bar in Carolina. Mexican restaurant in Shannock. Store at Wawaloam Campground, Gardner Road, Richmond. Diner, pizza shop, and grocery on Route 3. Several restaurants on Route 3 near starting point.

This is a scenic, relaxing ride through rural Rhode Island at its finest. The south-central portion of the state contains a harmonious mixture of woods and open land rising and falling across small ridges and valleys. A network of smooth, nearly traffic-free country roads traverses the region, providing ideal conditions for cycling. You'll pedal through the Arcadia Management Area, a large tract of woodland with a small beach. The long ride includes the old mill villages of Carolina, with its distinctive octagonal house, and Shannock, graced by stately old homes.

Start once again from Wyoming and turn onto a back road, which climbs gradually onto a forested ridge. Continue on to Route 112, where you'll see the Richmond Town House (the town hall) and the Bell School House, built in 1826. A mile ahead are the Washington County Fairgrounds, which host a traditional county fair every August.

Continuing south on Route 112, stop to observe the octagonal house on your left just past a crossroads. Just ahead cross the Pawcatuck River, where the fragile shell of what was once an old stone mill stands on the right. On the far side of the river is the village of

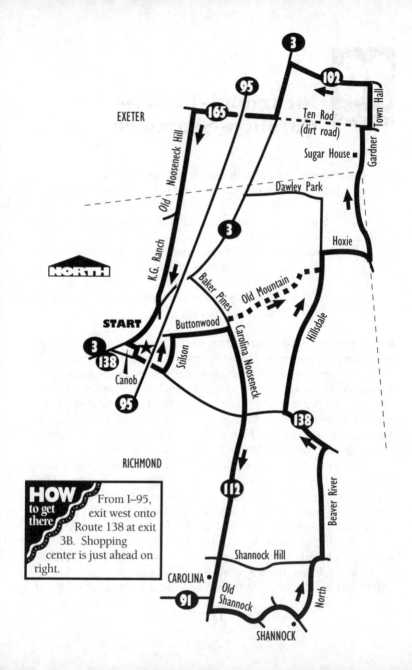

**DIREC-
TIONS**
for the ride

30 miles

- Left on Route 138 for 0.5 mile to Stilson Road on left, at traffic light. *Caution:* Busy road. Watch for traffic entering and exiting I–95.
- Left for 0.7 mile to end (Buttonwood Road).
- Right for 1 mile to end (Carolina Nooseneck Road, unmarked). Here the short ride turns left.
- Right for 1.7 miles to crossroads and stop sign (Route 138).
- Straight on Route 112 for 3.7 miles to Old Shannock Road (unmarked) on left, immediately after you go over a railroad bridge.
- Left for 0.6 mile to fork (Sand Plain Road bears right).
- Bear left for 0.6 mile to second left, North Road. (Horseshoe-shaped dam is 100 yards straight ahead.)
- Left for 1.2 miles to stop sign (merge right downhill).
- Bear right and just ahead turn left on Beaver River Road for 2.1 miles to end (Route 138).
- Left for 1.1 miles to Hillsdale Road on right.
- Right for 3.2 miles to Hoxie Road on right. It's 0.8 mile after James Trail on right.
- Right for 1 mile to stop sign at top of hill (merge right on Gardner Road.) You will turn sharply left here.
- Sharp left for 2.5 miles to end (Ten Rod Road). Pass Spring Hill Sugar House on left after 1.1 miles.
- Right and just ahead left on Town Hall Road for 0.6 mile to end (Route 102). *Caution:* Downhill stop at end.
- Left for 1.6 miles to end (Route 3).
- Left for 1.1 miles to blinking light (Route 165 on right).
- Right for 1.4 miles to Old Nooseneck Hill Road (unmarked) on left, at bottom of long hill (sign says ARCADIA MANAGEMENT AREA).
- Left for 1.8 miles to where main road curves sharply right and small road (K. G. Ranch Road, unmarked) goes straight.
- Straight for 2 miles to crossroads and stop sign (Route 3).
- Right for 0.8 mile to Canob Lane, which turns sharply left.
- Turn sharply left and just ahead take the first right. Go less than 0.2 mile to gas station on left just before end.

- Left through gas station to parking lot of shopping center.

18 miles

- Follow first 3 directions of long ride, to end of Buttonwood Road.
- Left for 0.2 mile to Old Mountain Road, which bears right.
- Bear right for 2.2 miles to end (Hillsdale Road, unmarked). Steep 0.4-mile hill at end.
- Left for 0.3 mile to Hoxie Road on right.
- Follow last 11 directions of long ride, beginning "Right for 1 mile to stop sign . . ."

Carolina, with a cluster of well-maintained frame houses and a small white church.

Just ahead turn east and bike through Shannock, a fine mill village with a grouping of gracious houses along the Pawcatuck River. Here the ride turns left, but if you go straight for a hundred yards you'll see a unique horseshoe-shaped dam. The stone shell of the mill, destroyed by fire, stands on your right just before the dam.

Turn north out of Shannock, pedaling on idyllic lanes through the valley of the Beaver River, actually just a small stream. Attractive farms, with stone walls and grazing horses, slope from the road down to the river. Head west briefly on Route 138 and then continue north on curving, wooded back roads, passing two small ponds and a cascading brook. A long, gradual climb brings you to the Spring Hill Sugar House, where maple syrup is processed and sold along with fresh cider in the fall. Descend sharply to Route 102 and then tackle the toughest hill of the ride as you turn west to Route 3. The well-named Middle of Nowhere Diner on Route 3 is a good spot for a snack.

The rest of the ride is mostly downhill. A smooth, steady descent on Route 165 brings you into the Arcadia Management Area, the largest state reservation in Rhode Island. It consists of forested hills laced with hiking trails and several small ponds. Turn south and pass Browning Mill Pond, which has a small beach. From here, a narrow lane through evergreen forests brings you back to Route 3 just north of Wyoming.

Wickford–Kingston

Number of miles:	15 (29 with Kingston extension)
Terrain:	Gently rolling, with several short hills. The longer ride has three additional moderate hills.
Start:	Town Dock, end of Main Street, Wickford.
Food:	Grocery in West Kingston on Route 138. Pizza shop at corner of Route 2 and Allenton Road. Restaurant on Route 1 near end. Several restaurant in downtown Wickford.
Facilities:	Portable toilet at start.

On this ride you'll explore a section of southern Rhode Island just inland from the west shore of Narragansett Bay. Both Wickford and Kingston are historic communities with handsome homes dating back to the early 1800s. In Kingston you will bike through the large, impressive campus of the University of Rhode Island, with its blend of traditional stone buildings and stark modern ones.

The picturesque harbor town of Wickford is a delightful place to start the ride. The town boasts an impressive collection of early nineteenth-century homes and hosts the state's largest art festival in July. As you leave the dock on Main Street, take a good look at all the houses, many with plaques indicating when they were built. Also on Main Street you pass the stately First Baptist Church, built in 1816. The spartan Old Narragansett Church, which dates from 1707 and is the oldest Episcopal church north of Virginia, is one block to your right.

Turn off Main Street and go through the center of town. On your right is the Wickford Diner, an authentic dining-car eatery sandwiched between two newer buildings. It's a good spot for a bite at the end of the ride. Just ahead cross the small bridge over the head of the

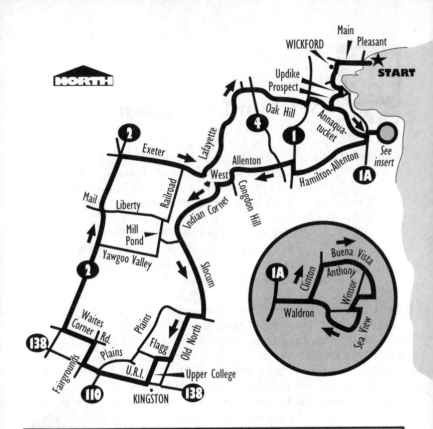

NORTH

WICKFORD

Main
Pleasant
START

Updike
Prospect

Oak Hill

Annaqua-
tucket

See
insert

Lafayette

2
Exeter

Allenton

West

Hamilton-Allenton

1A

Railroad

Mail

Liberty

Indian Corner

Congdon Hill

Mill
Pond

Yawgoo Valley

Slocum

2

Waites
Corner Rd.

Plains

Flagg

Old North

138

Plains

U.R.I.

Upper College

Fairgrounds

110

KINGSTON

138

Buena Vista

1A

Clinton

Anthony

Winsor

Waldron

Sea View

HOW to get there
From the north, head south on I–95 to Route 4 (exit on left). Go about 6 miles to the Route 102 South exit. Follow Route 102 about 2.5 miles to Route 1, at traffic light. Cross Route 1 and go 0.5 mile to fork (Route 1A bears right). Bear left for 0.2 mile, through downtown Wickford, to end. Turn right to dock.

From the southwest on I–95, exit south onto Route 102 for about 11 miles to Route 1, at traffic light. Cross Route 1 and go 0.5 mile to fork (Route 1A bears right). Bear left for 0.2 mile, through downtown Wickford, to end. Turn right to dock.

From the south, head north on Route 1 to Route 102 (traffic light). Right for 0.5 mile to fork (Route 1A bears right). Bear left for 0.2 mile, through downtown Wickford, to end. Turn right to dock.

**DIREC-
TIONS
for the ride**

29 miles

- Head away from dock on Main Street, and just ahead take first right on Pleasant Street. Go 0.3 mile to dead end, and backtrack to Main Street. You'll pass gracious homes that have frontage on Wickford Harbor.
- Right for 0.25 mile to stop sign (Brown Street, unmarked, on left).

To see Old Narragansett Church, take second right on Church Lane and go clockwise around the block back to Main Street.

- Left through downtown Wickford for 0.2 mile to wide fork (arched bridge on left).
- Left across bridge for 0.2 mile to first right, Updike Avenue.
- Bear right and just ahead bear right again at stop sign on Prospect Avenue. Go 0.6 mile to end (Annaquatucket Road, unmarked).
- Left for 1 mile to end (Route 1A), staying on main road.
- Left and just ahead right on Waldron Avenue. Go 0.3 mile to Clinton Drive, which bears left.
- Bear left for 0.2 mile to Anthony Drive on right, at DEAD END sign.
- Right for 0.2 mile to fork (Winsor Avenue bears right, Buena Vista Drive bears left).
- Bear left along water for 0.3 mile to end (Winsor Avenue, unmarked).
- Left for 0.1 mile to crossroads and stop sign (Waldron Avenue, unmarked).
- Turn left and follow paved road for 0.3 mile to stop sign (merge left on Waldron Avenue).
- Bear left for 0.4 mile to end (Route 1A).
- Left for 0.3 mile to second right (Hamilton-Allenton Road). You'll pass a small dam and fish ladder on left.
- Right for 1.5 miles to end (Route 1). *Caution:* Bumpy sections.
- Right for 0.2 mile to West Allenton Road (faded sign) on left.
- Left for 0.5 mile to traffic light at Route 4.
- Straight for 1 mile to stop sign where main road bears right uphill.
- Bear right for 0.5 mile to stop sign where Indian Corner Road turns left and Exeter Road bears right. Here the short ride bears right.

- Turn left for 3.4 miles to end (Stony Fort Road, unmarked).
- Right for 0.4 mile to Old North Road (unmarked) on left.
- Left for 0.9 mile to crossroads (Bean Farm Drive on left, Flagg Road on right).
- Right for 0.3 mile to Upper College Road on left.
- Left for 0.7 mile to end (Route 138).
- Right for 1.9 mile to second traffic light (Fairgrounds Road), immediately after railroad overpass.
- Right for 0.4 mile to crossroads and stop sign (Waites Corner Road).
- Left for 0.8 mile to fork.
- Bear right and just ahead turn right on Route 2. Go 4.1 miles to second crossroads (Exeter Road on right).
- Right for 1.8 miles to Lafayette Road on left, shortly after Dry Bridge Road on left. *Caution:* Watch for cracks.
- Left for 1.7 miles to fork while going uphill (Oak Hill Road bears right).
- Bear right and just ahead cross Route 4 at traffic light. Go 1.4 miles to end (Route 1, Tower Hill Road). *Caution:* Bumpy sections.
- Left for 0.3 mile to Annaquatucket Road on right.
- Right for 0.5 mile to Prospect Avenue on left. Notice striking sculpture of an Indian on left in front of a house.
- Left for 0.7 mile to Updike Avenue, which bears left at stop sign.
- Bear left and just ahead turn left at end (Route 1A). Go 0.2 mile to fork immediately after arched bridge.
- Right through downtown Wickford for 0.2 mile to end (Main Street).
- Right for 0.1 mile to first right (Gold Street).
- Right for 0.2 mile back to Main Street. Right to dock.

15 miles

- Follow first 20 directions of long ride, to stop sign where Indian Corner Road turns left and Exeter Road bears right.
- Bear right for 0.2 mile to Lafayette Road on right.

- Right for 1.7 miles to fork while going uphill (Oak Hill Road, unmarked, bears right).
- Follow last 8 directions of long ride.

---

boat-filled harbor. It's worth dismounting for a minute to savor the view of the town from the left side of the bridge. Just beyond the bridge is the redbrick North Kingstown Town Hall, built in 1888, on your left. (Wickford is part of North Kingstown.)

Two miles out of town make a small loop along the bay shore and take in the view of the Jamestown Bridge. The short ride now heads inland past small farms and estates hidden behind stone walls. The northbound leg on Lafayette Road is a delight as it winds over small rolling hills. Just after crossing Route 4, you will ride alongside Secret Lake, a good spot for a rest about 3 miles from the end.

The long ride turns south along Indian Corner Road, midway between Wickford and Kingston, and passes through extensive turf farms stretching to the horizon in a velvety green blanket. Slocum Road ascends gradually onto Kingston Hill, the long ridge where the village of Kingston and the University of Rhode Island are located. You approach Kingston on North Road, a byway so quiet that it is hard to believe that a major university with more than ten thousand students is a half mile away.

Kingston is refreshingly unique for a college town in that it is almost completely undeveloped. Even the main drag, Route 138, is uncommercialized and safe for riding. The commercial areas and most of the local population are centered in Wakefield, 4 miles south. After passing through the campus, turn right on Route 138. Notice the fine homes, most dating back to 1800, to your left at the intersection. About 2 miles ahead you pedal through West Kingston, passing the former Washington County Courthouse, a handsome granite building with a stately tower that was built in 1895. It is now a center for the arts. The graceful yellow railroad station, built in 1875 and recently restored, is on your left just past the arts center.

Continue on through more farmland to Route 2, a flat road with a good shoulder. You will follow Route 2 for several miles and then turn east onto Exeter Road, a pleasant road through wide stretches of gently rolling farmland. At the next intersection turn north on Lafayette Road, rejoining the short ride.

22 Bay and Beaches
Wakefield–Narragansett Pier–Bonnet Shores–Saunderstown

Number of miles: 17 (26 with Saunderstown extension)
Terrain: Gently rolling, with one vicious hill.
Start: Salt Pond Shopping Center, corner of Route 108 and Woodruff Avenue, Narragansett.
Food: Several stores and snack bars on Route 1A. Pizza at end.

On this ride you'll explore the southern reaches of Narragansett Bay where it empties into the Atlantic Ocean. The first half of the ride follows the coastline, looping around the scenic headland of Bonnet Shores and through the historic community of Saunderstown to the birthplace of Gilbert Stuart. The return trip heads inland past gentleman farms bordered by stone walls and rustic wooden fences.

The ride starts from the edge of Wakefield, the only large town in southern Rhode Island between Westerly and Narragansett Bay. Much of its economy is related to the University of Rhode Island, 4 miles to the north. From Wakefield, you head a short distance eastward to the gracious seaside town of Narragansett Pier. Just before you reach the ocean you pass the base of a water tower, originally 200 feet high, which was destroyed during the 1938 hurricane.

During the Gilded Age around the turn of the century, Narragansett Pier was a miniature Newport with huge Victorian resort hotels lining its seashore. Unfortunately, none remain. The town's major landmark from that era is the Towers, a stone building forming an arch across the road. This is the last remaining segment of the Narragansett Casino, designed in 1882 by Stanford White. Today the structure houses the Narragansett Tourist Information Center.

After pedaling underneath the Towers, head northward along the bay, going inland a few hundred feet and up onto a ridge overlooking the bay. After a few miles, you turn onto a side road that loops around Bonnet Shores, a rocky promontory jutting into Narragansett Bay with fine homes overlooking the water. The short ride then turns inland and descends to the Pettaquamscutt River (also called the Narrow River), a saltwater inlet about 2 miles west of the bay that runs parallel to it. You ride along the river for 2 miles; then you tackle a challenging hill as you turn inland from the riverbank. The last few miles continue inland past small farms and horse pastures.

The long ride continues farther north along the bay to the historic community of Saunderstown. From the hillside, superb views of the bay and the graceful span of the Jamestown Bridge unfold before you. You pass Casey Farm, an unspoiled tract of land that has been cultivated since the Revolution. Administered by the Society for the Preservation of New England Antiquities, it has a fine collection of period furniture and memorabilia and is open from June through October. Just past the farm turn inland to view another historic landmark, the birthplace of Gilbert Stuart. The country's famous portrait painter, best known for his portrait of George Washington on the dollar bill, was born here in 1755. Next to the home where he was born is the first snuff mill in the United States, built in 1751 by the artist's father.

A tough hill leads from the birthplace to Route 1. Cross this highway and return to Wakefield on back roads passing attractive farms. You'll ride through the historic village of Peace Dale, which is adjacent to Wakefield. In the center of town is a cluster of handsome stone buildings from the mid-to-late nineteenth century; be sure to notice the elegant library, built in 1891, on the right. Across the street is the Museum of Primitive Art and Culture; hours vary depending on staff volunteers.

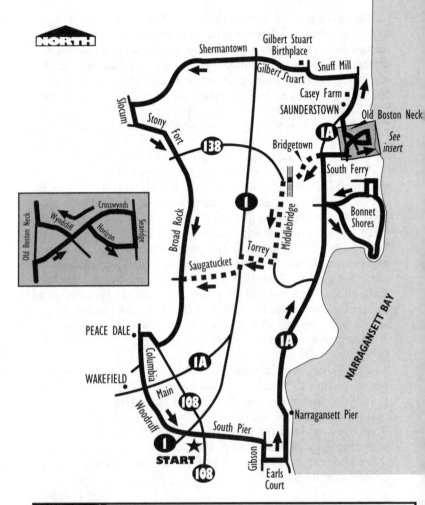

NORTH

Shermantown

Gilbert Stuart Birthplace

Gilbert Stuart

Snuff Mill

Casey Farm

SAUNDERSTOWN

Slocum

Stony

Fort

138

Bridgetown

Old Boston Neck

See insert

1A

South Ferry

Bonnet Shores

Broad Rock

1

Middlebridge

Torrey

Saugatucket

NARRAGANSETT BAY

PEACE DALE

Columbia

1A

WAKEFIELD

Main

108

Woodruff

South Pier

Narragansett Pier

1

★
START

108

Gibson

Earls Court

Insert: Old Boston Neck · Crosswynds · Wyndcliff · Horizon · Searidge

HOW to get there

From the north, take Route 1 to the Route 108, Point Judith, Scarborough exit. Bear right at end of ramp; shopping center is just ahead on right.

From the south, take Route 1 to the Narragansett–Point Judith exit. Turn right at end of exit ramp and shopping center is just ahead on right.

DIREC-TIONS for the ride

26 miles

- Left on Route 108 for 0.1 mile to traffic light.
- Right on South Pier Road for 1.2 miles to crossroads and stop sign (Gibson Avenue on right).
- Right for 0.2 mile to Earls Court on left.
- Left for 0.3 mile to end (Ocean Road), at stop sign.
- Left for 0.9 mile to end, at traffic light. You'll go underneath the Towers.
- Bear right along water on Route 1A North. Go 3.8 miles to traffic light (Wampum Road on left, Bonnet Shores Road on right).
- Turn right and just ahead bear right at fork. Go 2.1 miles to where main road curves sharply left and smaller road bears right along the water. *Caution:* Bumpy spots.
- Bear right. After 0.2 mile, road turns 90 degrees left. Go less than 0.2 mile to first left (Webster Avenue).
- Left for 0.2 mile to third crossroads and stop sign (Bonnet Shores Road).
- Right for 0.7 mile to traffic light (Route 1A, Boston Neck Road).
- Right for 0.8 mile to traffic light (Bridgetown Road on left, South Ferry Road on right). Here the short ride turns left.
- Right for 0.4 mile to crossroads (Ray Trainor Drive on right, Old Boston Neck Road on left).
- Left for 0.25 mile to Crosswynds Drive on right.
- Right for 0.25 mile to Horizon Drive (second right).
- Right for 0.25 mile to end (Searidge Drive).
- Left and just ahead left again on Crosswynds Drive. Go 0.3 mile to crossroads and stop sign (Wyndcliff Drive).
- Right for less than 0.2 mile to end (Old Boston Neck Road, unmarked).
- Right for 0.5 mile to diagonal crossroads and stop sign (Route 1A). *Caution:* Bumpy sections.
- Bear right for 1.3 miles to Snuff Mill Road on left.
- Left for 1 mile to Gilbert Stuart Road on left (sign may say GILBERT STUART MUSEUM). *Caution:* Steep, curving descent.
- Turn left. Gilbert Stuart's birthplace and snuff mill are on right just

ahead at bottom of hill. Continue 1.1 miles to Route 1, at stop sign. You'll climb very steeply for 0.3 mile.

- Straight (*Caution* here) for 3.1 miles to end (Slocum Road, unmarked).
- Left for 0.25 mile to end (Stony Fort Road, unmarked).
- Left for 1.4 miles to end (Route 138, Mooresfield Road).
- Jog right and immediately left onto Broad Rock Road (*Caution* here). Go 2 miles to crossroads and stop sign (Saugatucket Road).
- Straight for 1.2 miles to end (Route 108, Kingstown Road).
- Right for 0.3 mile to end, in Peace Dale (Route 108 turns right). The Museum of Primitive Art and Culture is on left at end.
- Left on Columbia Street for 0.3 mile to fork (River Street bears right).
- Bear left (still Columbia Street) for 0.3 mile to traffic light (Main Street). Stedman's Bicycle Shop on far right corner.
- Straight for 1.1 miles to shopping center on right.

17 miles

- Follow first 11 directions of long ride, to junction of Route 1A and Bridgetown Road.
- Left for 0.8 mile to Middlebridge Road (unmarked) on left, 100 yards after bridge.
- Left for 1.6 miles to Torrey Road on right.
- Right for 0.5 mile to Route 1 (huff, puff, groan).
- Turn right. Just ahead make U-turn at traffic light, using ramp to cross highway at right angles. Go 0.2 mile to Saugatucket Road on right, at blinking light.
- Right for 1.2 miles to crossroads and stop sign (Broad Rock Road).
- Left for 1.2 miles to end (Route 108, Kingstown Road).
- Follow last 4 directions of long ride.

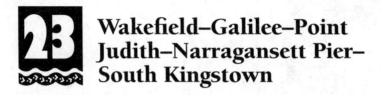

Wakefield–Galilee–Point Judith–Narragansett Pier–South Kingstown

Number of miles:	16 (28 with South Kingstown extension)
Terrain:	Flat, with one monstrous hill and two moderate ones on the long ride.
Start:	Salt Pond Shopping Center, corner of Route 108 and Woodruff Avenue, Narragansett.
Food:	Snack bars in Galilee. Aunt Carrie's, corner of Route 108 and Ocean Road. Great seafood! Several snack bars near beaches, open during the summer. Snack bar on Middlebridge Road (long ride). Burger King and McDonald's on Tower Hill Road, about a mile north of starting point.
Facilities:	Rest room across the road from Block Island ferry dock.
Caution:	During the summer, traffic in the beach areas is very heavy. Best time to ride is early in the morning, late afternoon, or during the off-season.

On this ride you'll explore the midpoint of Rhode Island's southern coast, where the shoreline turns abruptly northward at Point Judith. Views of the ocean abound as you head to the picturesque fishing village of Galilee and then south to the tip of the peninsula. Follow the shore past gracious waterfront homes to Narragansett Pier, where you'll pedal beneath the arch of the Towers, an architectural landmark designed by Stanford White.

As in Ride 23, the ride starts just outside of Wakefield. Head south on Route 108 down the Point Judith peninsula, taking advantage of the wide shoulder along this road, which is very busy on beach days. You'll pass Fishermen's Memorial State Park (a camp-

ground with some athletic fields). Just ahead, as you turn west toward Galilee, a panorama of broad salt marshes unfolds before you. In the distance you can see Point Judith Pond, the long saltwater inlet that separates Point Judith from the mainland. Galilee, an active fishing port that has not been overly commercialized, is the main terminal for the ferry to Block Island. Outside of Galilee, Roger W. Wheeler State Beach (also called Sand Hill Cove Beach), is the best spot on the ride for a swim.

Bike to the tip of Point Judith, a broad grassy promontory commanded by a lighthouse and Coast Guard station, where the grounds (but not the buildings) are open to the public. The northward run along the coast road to Narragansett Pier is bicycle heaven. You pass crowded Scarborough State Beach, where most of Rhode Island's teenagers will be found on hot weekend afternoons, and elegant cedar-shingled homes overlooking the sea. Short dead-end roads afford even better views of the rocky coast.

You continue through the pleasant seaside community of Narragansett Pier and under the stone arch of the Towers. Just ahead the short ride turns inland and passes another landmark, a magnificent wooden sculpture of a Narragansett Indian chief. The South County Museum, with exhibits of early Rhode Island rural life and industries, is off Route 1A just north of the point where the short ride heads inland.

The long ride continues north to the Narrow River (also called the Pettaquamscutt River), a slender saltwater inlet paralleling the coastline, which you'll cross twice on picturesque bridges, first on Route 1A and then on Middlebridge Road. The one tough climb of the ride awaits you when you turn inland from the riverbank. The rest of the tour passes through a typical South County landscape of fine homes, woodlots, little ponds, and small farms bordered by stone walls and shade trees.

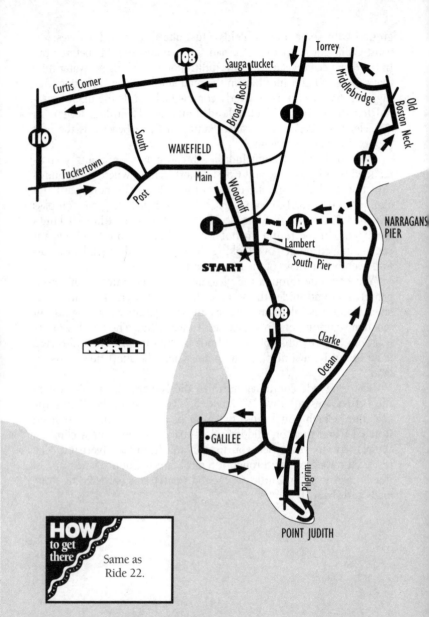

108

Torrey

Curtis Corner

Sauga tucket

Middlebridge

Old Boston Neck

Broad Rock

1

110

South

WAKEFIELD

Tuckertown

Main

Woodruff

1A

Post

1

1A

NARRAGANS
PIER

Lambert

South Pier

START

108

Clarke

NORTH

Ocean

GALILEE

Pilgrim

POINT JUDITH

HOW
to get
there

Same as
Ride 22.

- Right on Route 108 for 3.6 miles to divided road on right at traffic light (sign says GALILEE, GREAT ISLAND, BLOCK ISLAND BOAT). You'll go straight at several traffic lights on this stretch.
- Right for 1.1 miles to crossroads and stop sign. An observation tower on your right at the intersection provides a fine view of a salt mash. At the crossroads the ride goes left, but you can turn right to go around Great Island, with fine views of Point Judith Pond. (This adds 3 miles to ride.)
- Left for 0.3 mile to where the main road curves sharply left. Here the ride curves left, but straight ahead is popular George's Restaurant and the little Salty Brine State Beach. The name refers not to the water, but to a well-loved radio personality famous for booming out "No school, Foster–Glocester".
- Curve left for 0.2 mile and then continue straight, following sign to Sand Hill Cove. Go 1.3 miles to end (Route 108).
- Right for 0.3 mile to crossroads and stop sign (Ocean Road, unmarked).
- Turn right and stay on main road for 0.9 mile to Point Judith Coast Guard Station, at end. Leave your bike outside the gate to the station (and lock it) and enjoy the views from the grounds on foot. The NO VEHICLES sign at the gate is taken literally by Coast Guard personnel. Although the sign says "Authorized personnel only," a Coast Guard officer assured me that it refers to the buildings and not the grounds, and that visitors are welcome on foot. The slanted wooden platforms on your right as you enter the grounds are used for testing DuPont paint samples.
- Backtrack 0.5 mile to Pilgrim Avenue on right.
- Right for 0.2 mile to Calef Avenue on left.
- Left along ocean for 0.4 mile to end (Ocean Road, unmarked). *Caution:* Last 0.1 mile is bumpy.
- Right for 4.8 miles to end, at traffic light just past Towers.

After about a mile you'll pass Scarborough State Beach. If it's not a beach day and there are no pedestrians, you can ride along the sidewalk next to the ocean. If you bear right on Newton Avenue just after Ocean Road curves sharply right (it's 1.6 miles beyond Scarborough State Beach), there is a spectacular view of rocky shoreline. Hazard Avenue, another small road 0.3 mile after Newton Avenue, leads to another fine ocean view.

- Bear right for 1 block to another light where Narragansett Avenue turns left. Here the short ride turns left. South County Museum is 0.2 mile straight ahead, then left on dirt road for 0.25 mile.
- Straight on Route 1A for 1.2 miles to Old Boston Neck Road on right, immediately after bridge over Narrow River.
- Turn right and stay on main road for 0.5 mile back to Route 1A (Boston Neck Road), at stop sign.
- Cross Route 1A diagonally. Go 0.3 mile to Middlebridge Road on left, at stop sign.
- Left for 1 mile to Torrey Road on left.
- Left for 0.5 mile to end (Route 1). Hill!
- Turn right. Just ahead make U-turn at traffic light, using ramp to cross highway at right angles. Go 0.2 mile to Saugatucket Road on right, at blinking light.
- Right for 5 miles to end (Route 110, Ministerial Road), going straight at three crossroads.
- Left for 1.3 miles to blinking light (Wordens Pond Road on right, Tuckertown Road on left).
- Left for 2.4 miles to end (Post Road).
- Left for 1.4 miles to traffic light (Woodruff Avenue on right). You'll go through downtown Wakefield. Stedman's Bicycle Shop is on your right at the intersection.
- Right for 1.1 miles to shopping center on right.

16 miles

- Follow first 11 directions of long ride, to second traffic light after you go underneath the Towers.
- Left for almost 0.2 mile to another light (Route 1A South, Narragansett Avenue on right).

- Right for 1 mile to Lambert Street on left, opposite redbrick church on right. (Indian statue on right after 0.3 mile at traffic light.)
- Left for 0.3 mile to end (South Pier Road, unmarked).
- Right and immediately left at traffic light. *Caution:* Busy intersection. Shopping center is on right.

The Jonnycake Ride
Kingston–Usquepaug–Shannock

Number of miles:	17 (23 with Shannock extension)
Terrain:	Gently rolling, with one hill. The long ride has several short hills.
Start:	University of Rhode Island tennis courts, Route 138, Kingston.
Food:	Grocery on Route 138, West Kingston. Farm stand and pizza shop on Route 138. Mexican restaurant in Shannock, and sandwich shop just beyond it. *Caution:* Route 138 is busy. Start early to avoid traffic.

The area just west of Kingston is delightful for bicycling, with dozens of traffic-free back roads weaving across the rural countryside. A highlight of this ride is the Kenyon Grist Mill in Usquepaug, which grinds corn and other grains into flour (including Rhode Island's unique jonnycake flour) using the same methods as when the mill was built in 1886.

The ride begins by heading through West Kingston, where you'll pass the railroad station built in 1875. You'll follow back roads along brilliantly green turf farms, white farmhouses, and stretches of woodland toward Usquepaug. You pass Peter Pots Kilns, a manufacturer of fine ceramics and stoneware housed in an old mill. The gristmill is a mile ahead; it is open by appointment (phone 401–783–4054). The jonnycake (a corruption of "journeycake") is a Rhode Island specialty, made from cornmeal and introduced by the Narragansett Indians to the early settlers. A small shop across the road sells bags of the mill's stone-ground products. The little pond and dam behind the mill provide the waterpower that still turns the millstones.

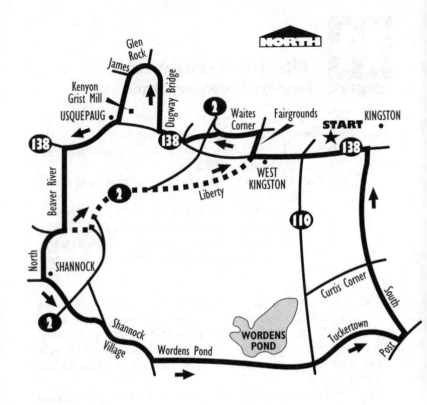

HOW to get there

From the north, head south on I–95 and Route 4 to Route 102 North (exit 5B) to Route 2 South to Route 138. Turn left for 2 miles to parking lot on left, just past tennis courts.

From the west, exit east from I–95 onto Route 138. Go about 9 miles to Route 110 on right, at traffic light. Continue on Route 138 for 0.7 mile to parking lot on left. From the east, head west on Route 138 to Route 108 on left. Continue straight for 0.9 mile to parking lot on right, at bottom of hill just before tennis courts.

- Right on Route 138 for 0.7 mile to traffic light (Route 110 on left).
- Straight for 0.6 mile to traffic light immediately after railroad overpass (Fairgrounds Road). Notice the railroad station on your left.
- Right for 0.4 mile to crossroads and stop sign (Waites Corner Road).
- Left for 0.8 mile to fork.
- Bear left and just ahead cross Route 2. Go 0.5 mile to end (Route 138, Usquepaug Road).
- Bear right on Route 138 (don't turn 90 degrees right on Sand Turn Road). Go 1.1 miles to Dugway Bridge Road on right (sign may say PETER POTS POTTERY).
- Right for 1.1 miles to Glen Rock Road on left, immediately after small bridge.
- Left for 0.4 mile to fork (James Trail bears right).
- Bear left for 0.9 mile to stop sign. The Kenyon Grist Mill is on your left just before the stop sign. Notice the dam immediately after the mill.
- Bear right (almost straight) for 0.2 mile to end (Route 138).
- Right for 1.2 miles to second left, Beaver River Road.
- Left for 2 miles to end, at yield sign. Here the short ride turns left.
- Right for 0.1 mile to fork (North Road bears left).
- Bear left for 1.2 miles to end (Shannock Village Road), in Shannock.
- Left for 0.6 mile to crossroads and stop sign (Route 2). Sandwich shop on left at intersection.
- Straight for 1.5 miles to Wordens Pond Road on left, at stop sign.
- Left for 2.9 miles to blinking light (Route 110, Ministerial Road).
- Straight for 2.4 miles to end (Post Road).
- Left for 0.2 mile to South Road on left.
- Left for 1.6 miles to crossroads and stop sign (Curtis Corner Road).
- Straight for 1.8 miles to end (Route 138, Kingstown Road).
- Left for 0.8 mile to parking lot on right, just past bottom of hill.

17 miles

- Follow first 12 directions of long ride, to end of Beaver River Road.
- Left for 0.4 mile to wide fork at top of hill.
- Left for 0.2 mile to end (merge left on Route 2).
- Bear left for 1.8 miles to Liberty Lane on right.
- Bear right for 1.8 miles to traffic light (Route 138, Kingstown Road).
- Right for 0.6 mile to traffic light (Route 110 on right).
- Straight for 0.7 mile to parking lot on left.

Just past Usquepaug head south on Beaver River Road. This is the kind of lane you see photographed in country magazines, with ribbons of pastureland bordered by stone walls and rows of impressive shade trees. To your left, the small Beaver River ripples at the edge of the fields. A couple of miles ahead is the site of the Great Swamp Fight, which took place in 1675 during King Philip's War and resulted in the near annihilation of the Narragansett Indians. A monument commemorating the event stands off Route 2 on a dirt road. From here it's a short ride back to West Kingston along another narrow rustic road, with the University of Rhode Island just ahead.

The long ride heads a little farther south, following the Beaver River along another picture-book lane. Suddenly you round a bend, and the antique mill village of Shannock lies before you. A cluster of gracious white homes with black shutters overlooks the Pawcatuck River, which flows over a unique horseshoe-shaped dam. Only a shell remains of the mill, a victim of fire.

A couple of miles beyond Shannock, a gentle descent brings you to the shore of Wordens Pond. After a relaxing ride along the water, head again through prosperous South County farms interspersed with forests. At the end, you'll finish with a flourish as you zip down Kingston Hill.

South County
Kingston–Shannock–
Charlestown–Matunuck

Number of miles:	19 (32 with Shannock–Charlestown extension)
Terrain:	Gently rolling, with several moderate hills.
Start:	University of Rhode Island tennis courts, Route 138, Kingston.
Food:	Sandwich shop on Route 2. Mexican restaurant in Shannock. Grocery and ice cream shop in Charlestown. Grocery in Matunuck.

The southern third of Rhode Island west of Narragansett Bay consists of Washington County, which most state residents affectionately call South County. This is an area of unique beauty. The coastline, containing some of the finest beaches in the Northeast, extends along a series of narrow spits of land with the ocean on the south and, on the north, salt ponds swarming with birds. Inland is a refreshingly varied landscape of farmland and wooded hills, interspersed with ponds, swamps, and picturesque mill villages.

The ride starts from the lower edge of the University of Rhode Island campus at the bottom of Kingston Hill. Head south for several miles on Route 110, one of the more pleasant numbered routes in the state for cycling. You'll cross the defunct Narragansett Pier Railroad, a single-track, narrow-gauge line that once transported thousands of beachgoers from the Kingston train station to the ocean before the automobile took its place. It is now under construction as a bicycle path. Soon you pass unspoiled Larkin Pond and then enjoy a relaxing ride along the shore of Wordens Pond, the second largest freshwater lake in the state. After a few miles you'll pass the Perryville Trout Hatchery, which is open to visitors Monday through Friday from 10:00 A.M. to 3:00 P.M.

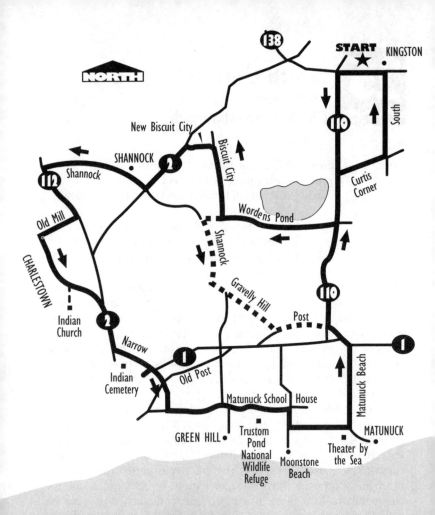

NORTH

138

START KINGSTON

110

South

New Biscuit City

SHANNOCK

2

Biscuit City

110

Curtis Corner

112 Shannock

Wordens Pond

Old Mill

CHARLESTOWN

Shannock

Gravelly Hill

110

2

Indian Church

Post

1

Narrow

1

Old Post

Matunuck Beach

Indian Cemetery

Matunuck School House

MATUNUCK

GREEN HILL

Trustom Pond National Wildlife Refuge

Moonstone Beach

Theater by the Sea

HOW to get there

Same as Ride 24.

- Right on Route 138 for 0.7 mile to traffic light (Route 110 on left).
- Left for 3.8 miles to crossroads and blinking light (Wordens Pond Road on right).
- Right for 2.6 miles to Biscuit City Road on right. Here the short ride goes straight.
- Right for 1.3 miles to wide unmarked road on left, at bottom of hill (sign may say TO ROUTE 2).
- Left for 0.4 mile to end (Route 2).
- Left for 0.6 mile to crossroads (Shannock Road, unmarked).
- Right for 1.8 miles to end (Route 112). *Caution:* Bumpy sections.
- Left for 0.9 mile to Old Mill Road on right.
- Right for 2.4 miles to Route 2, at end. (Dirt road on right, after 2 miles, at top of hill, leads 0.7 mile to Indian Church. Follow dirt road to fork, and bear right for 50 yards to church.)
- Bear right for 1 mile to Narrow Lane on left.
- Left for 1.3 miles to Route 1. (After 0.7 mile, Indian cemetery is on right almost at bottom of hill and immediately before a blocked-off paved road. Turn sharply right onto dirt path for 0.2 mile.)
- Right for 0.2 mile to U-turn slot in median strip.
- Make U-turn and go 0.2 mile to first exit (sign says CHARLESTOWN BEACH). *Caution* making U-turn.
- Bear right for 0.4 mile to end (Matunuck Schoolhouse Road, unmarked).
- Left for 1.4 miles to fork (Green Hill Beach Road bears right). Here the ride bears left, but to visit Green Hill Beach, bear right instead of left for 1 mile.
- Bear left (still Matunuck Schoolhouse Road) for 1.6 miles to crossroads and stop sign (Moonstone Beach Road).
- Turn right. After 0.4 mile, paved road turns 90 degrees left (dirt road goes straight ahead for 0.4 mile to Moonstone Beach). Continue on paved road 1.1 miles to end (Matunuck Beach Road). At the end the ride turns left, but to visit Matunuck Beach, turn right for 100 yards to entrance; the main road continues along the ocean for 0.6 mile.

- Left for 1.4 miles to Route 1.
- Turn right and go to U-turn slot in median strip just ahead.
- Make U-turn and go 0.4 mile to first exit (sign says POST ROAD, PERRYVILLE). *Caution* making U-turn.
- Bear right for 0.3 mile to crossroads and stop sign (Route 110, Ministerial Road).
- Right for 2.1 miles to crossroads and blinking light.
- Straight for 1.3 miles to Curtis Corner Road on right.
- Right for 1.6 miles to crossroads and stop sign (South Road).
- Left for 1.8 miles to end (Route 138).
- Left for 0.8 mile to parking lot on right, just past bottom of hill.

19 miles

- Follow first 3 directions of long ride, to Biscuit City Road on right.
- Straight for 0.3 mile to end (Shannock Road).
- Left for 1.3 miles to stop sign where Gravelly Hill Road goes straight and Shannock Road bears right.
- Straight for 1.5 miles to end (Post Road, unmarked).
- Left for 0.9 mile to crossroads and stop sign (Route 110, Ministerial Road).
- Left for 2.1 miles to crossroads and blinking light.
- Follow last 4 directions of long ride.

To finish the ride, follow the southern half of Route 110 and then take side roads into Kingston past small farms and older homes set back from the roadway on wooded lots. When you come to Route 138 in Kingston, notice the lovely historic houses, handsome white church, and the Old Washington County Jail (now headquarters of the local Historical Society) gracing both sides of the road. Breeze down Kingston Hill at the end of your ride.

The long ride heads farther west after the ride along Wordens Pond. There is a gradual climb followed by a gentle descent to the headwaters of the Pawcatuck River, which flows from the pond to the southwestern corner of the state. You parallel the river briefly and come to Route 2, where you'll see the large concrete mill building of Kenyon Industries. This is a major manufacturer of coated nylon for bike bags, panniers, and tents, and waterproofing seam-sealer. Just ahead wind through Shannock, a museum-piece mill village of rambling wooden homes with broad porches and black shutters. The Pawcatuck River flows over an unusual horseshoe-shaped dam and past the burned-out shell of the mill.

A few miles beyond Shannock, take wooded back roads through the tribal homeland of Narragansett Indians in Charlestown. The tribe would like to construct a casino here (it's one of several proposed sites) if the Narragansetts can get both legislative and voter approval, which appears unlikely. Tucked away on a dirt road off the route is the Narragansett Indian Church, a small stone structure built in 1859. Off Narrow Lane, hidden on a narrow dirt road, is the Royal Indian Burial Ground. It is marked by a single white gravestone. Just ahead you cross Route 1 and parallel the southern coast for several miles.

After crossing Route 1, you enter the broad meadows of the coastal plain. The ocean lies about a mile south, with several side roads leading down to the beaches. The ecology of the shoreline is too fragile to support a road directly along the coast, so to get down to the beach you will have to ride a small additional distance. There are several beaches you can visit. The first is Green Hill Beach, with a community of attractive summer homes on the gentle hillside overlooking the beach. Two miles east is Moonstone Beach, completely undeveloped and a traditional spot for skinny-dipping. Between these two beaches is Trustom Pond National Wildlife Refuge, a wonderful area for bird watching. The next beach is Matunuck, the most built up and commercialized of the three. Between Moonstone and Matunuck is the popular summer theater, Theater by the Sea.

At Matunuck turn northward for the trip back to Kingston. After crossing Route 1 you'll rejoin the short ride at the southern end of Route 110.

South County
Chariho Area

Number of miles:	17 (25 with East Beach loop)
Terrain:	Rolling, with a tough hill on Woodville Road and on Buckeye Brook Road.
Start:	Chariho High School, Hope Valley Road in Richmond, Rhode Island.
Food:	Grocery at junction of Routes 91 and 216 West near Bradford. Doughnut shop in Bradford. Pizza shop and grocery at junction of Routes 216 and 1, for the long ride.

Just northeast of Westerly, almost at the southwest corner of Rhode Island, are the three small South County towns of Charlestown, Richmond, and Hopkinton, collectively called Chariho. The region abounds with winding rural roads that promise carefree cycling.

At the beginning of the ride there is the lovely village of Woodville, where three old, imposing houses stand opposite a fine little dam and millpond. A steady climb out of the village brings you onto a wooded ridge, where you turn south on Tomaquag Road, a twisting, narrow back road. The forest suddenly thins out as you begin a glorious descent from the ridge, enjoying the sweeping view of the valley on your right.

Continue on into Charlestown, a thoroughly rural town except for some summer colonies along the splendid southern coast. Since the bicycle boom of the 1970s, Charlestown has become a center for competitive cycling in New England. Time trials, an event in which participants race a set distance (usually 10 miles) against the clock rather than against each other, are held weekly on Route 1. With its wide shoulders and U-turn slots in the median strip, this highway is

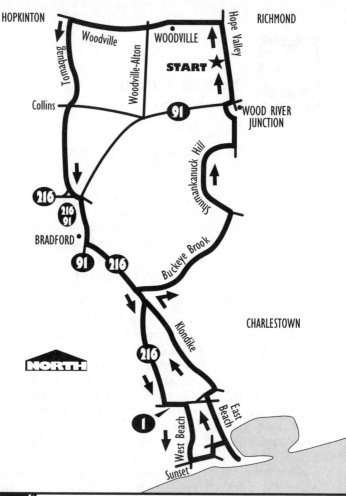

HOPKINTON
RICHMOND
Hope Valley
Woodville
WOODVILLE
Woodville-Alton
START ★
Tomaquag
Collins
91
WOOD RIVER JUNCTION
Shumankanuck Hill
216
216 91
BRADFORD
91
216
Buckeye Brook
CHARLESTOWN
Klondike
216
East Beach
1
West Beach
Sunset

NORTH

HOW to get there From the north, exit west from I–95 onto Route 138. Go 1.1 miles to traffic light where Route 3 goes straight and Route 138 turns right. Bear left here on Mechanic Street and go 4 miles to school on the right.

From the south, exit north from I–95 onto Route 3, just past the state line. Go 1 mile to crossroads (Clarks Falls Road on left, Woodville Road on right). Turn right at crossroads and go 4 miles to end. Turn right at end, and go 0.8 mile to school on right.

- Left out of parking lot for 0.8 mile to first left (Woodville Road, unmarked).
- Left for 1.4 miles to crossroads and stop sign (Woodville-Alton Road).
- Straight for 1.4 miles to Tomaquag Road on left, just as you start to go down a hill.
- Left for 1.3 miles to crossroads and stop sign (Collins Road).
- Straight for 2.1 miles to fork at bottom of hill (James Road bears right).
- Bear left and just ahead turn left at end (Route 216). Go 0.3 mile to crossroads and stop sign (Route 91).
- Right for 0.9 mile to where Route 216 (Church Street) turns left and Route 91 goes straight.
- Left for 1.3 miles to Buckeye Brook Road on left. Here the short ride turns left.
- Straight for 0.3 mile to fork (main road bears right).
- Bear right for 2.2 miles to end (Route 1).
- Left (*Caution*) for 0.4 mile to West Beach Road on right (sign says QUONOCHONTAUG).
- Right for 1 mile to crossroads (Sunset Drive on right, Sea Breeze Avenue on left).
- Left for 0.4 mile to Midland Road on left, immediately after stop sign (private road goes straight).
- Left for 0.2 mile to crossroads and stop sign.
- Right on main road for 0.2 mile to end (East Beach Road, unmarked).
- Right for 0.3 mile to ocean.
- Make a U-turn at ocean and go 1.1 miles to Route 1.
- Cross Route 1 (*Caution:* Walk bike across median). Go straight for 50 feet to end, at church.
- Right for 0.2 mile to first left (sign says BURLINGAME STATE PARK, visible from opposite direction).
- Left for 0.2 mile to park entrance road, which bears right.

- Straight on Klondike Road (unmarked) for 2.4 miles to end (merge right on Route 216).
- Bear right for 0.3 mile to Buckeye Brook Road on right.
- Right for 2.8 miles to end (Shumankanuck Hill Road, unmarked).
- Left for 2 miles to end (Kings Factory Road, unmarked).
- Left for 1 mile to end (Route 91).
- Right for 0.3 mile to crossroads (Switch Road on left).
- Left for 0.8 mile to school on left.

17 miles

- Follow first 8 directions of long ride, to Buckeye Brook Road.
- Left for 2.8 miles to end (Shumankanuck Hill Road, unmarked).
- Follow last 4 directions of long ride.

---

ideal for the event. Races are occasionally held at Ninigret Park, which is 2 miles east of the route, off Route 1. Most of these events are open to novices. If you're interested, inquire at King's Cyclery in Westerly (401–322–6005) or at Stedman's Bike Shop in Wakefield (401–789–8664).

Buckeye Brook Road winds through wooded Burlingame State Park. You climb onto a ridge and enjoy a fast descent with a fine view. Just before the end, you enter the tiny village of Wood River Junction.

Instead of turning onto Buckeye Brook Road, the long ride continues south to the ocean along Quonochontaug Neck, a peninsula between two large salt ponds. Follow the paved road to East Beach, a fine example of the string of barrier beaches forming Rhode Island's southern shore. Beyond the road's end is the Ninigret Conservation Area, a narrow, unspoiled strip of land over 3 miles long that forms a frail barrier between the sea and Ninigret Pond. Heading north from the ocean, you pass the entrance to Burlingame State Park, a large expanse of woodland and swamp. The entrance road leads for about a mile to a campground and a freshwater beach on Watchaug Pond. After winding through the woods for 2 miles on a narrow secondary road, turn onto Buckeye Brook Road to rejoin the short ride.

Cows and Casinos
Hopkinton–North Stonington, Connecticut

Number of miles: 17 (29 with Foxwoods extension)
         Terrain: Rolling, with one long hill and several shorter
                   ones.
           Start: Commuter parking lot, Route 216, in North
                   Stonington, Connecticut. It's just west of I–95 at
                   the state line.
            Food: Restaurant opposite starting point. Convenience
                   store in North Stonington. Restaurants at Fox-
                   woods Casino. There are no food stops along the
                   route of the short ride.

The area straddling the southern part of the Rhode Island–Connecticut
border is rolling and inspiringly beautiful. It is a region of pristine villages, high ridges with superb views from their summits, and broad
expanses of farmland full of cows and horses. This ride, most of
which winds through the lovely rural town of North Stonington,
Connecticut, abounds with smooth, traffic-free back roads where the
effort of some hills will be counterbalanced by two glorious descents.
The long ride goes past Foxwoods Casino, which is worth visiting as
a social and architectural phenomenon (and to see the impressive Indian museum), even if you don't gamble.

   The ride starts at the state line and passes through Hopkinton,
Rhode Island, for the first few miles. Clustered near the main crossroads of the attractive village are a small white church, the town hall,
the impressive Heritage Playhouse, and several lovely homes, including one dated 1780. A mile west of the village you enter Connecticut
and enjoy a long descent to a prosperous dairy farm, with sweeping
views of neighboring hillsides. Just ahead is the tiny hamlet of Clarks

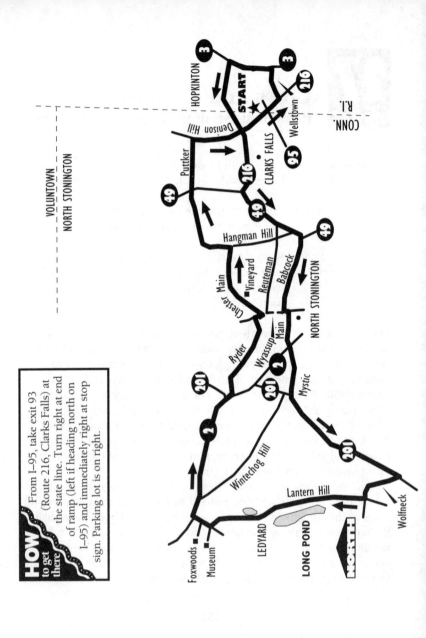

HOW to get there

From I-95, take exit 93 (Route 216, Clarks Falls) at the state line. Turn right at end of ramp (left if heading north on I-95) and immediately right at stop sign. Parking lot is on right.

VOLUNTOWN
NORTH STONINGTON

CONN.
R.I.

HOPKINTON
3
3
216
START
Wellstown
95
Denison Hill
CLARKS FALLS
216
Puttker
49
49
Hangman Hill
49
Chester Main
Vineyard
Reuteman
Babcock
NORTH STONINGTON
Ryder
Wyassup
Main
201
201
1
Mystic
2
201
Wintechog Hill
Lantern Hill
Wolfneck
Foxwoods
Museum
LEDYARD
LONG POND
NORTH

- Left out of lot, and immediately left at stop sign, going underneath I–95. Go 0.6 mile to Wellstown Road on left. *Caution:* Bumps and potholes.
- Left (it's a fairly sharp left) for 0.6 mile to end (Route 3).
- Left for 1.5 miles to crossroads, in Hopkinton (Woodville Road on right, Clarks Falls Road on left).
- Left for 2.3 miles to crossroads and stop sign (Denison Hill Road).
- Straight for 1.3 miles to stop sign (Route 49 bears right and turns left).
- Left for 1.3 miles to fork (main road bears left, Babcock Road bears right).
- Bear right for 1.7 miles to end (Wyassup Road). Here the short ride turns right, but if you're doing the short ride it's worth turning left into North Stonington.
- Left for 0.1 mile to Main Street on right, in North Stonington. Take a look at the stream that flows behind the yellow gristmill on the far side of the intersection.
- Right for 0.5 mile to traffic light (Route 2).
- Straight on Mystic Road, passing convenience store on left. Stay on main road for 3.9 miles to Wolfneck Road, which turns sharply right.
- Right for 1 mile to crossroads and stop sign (Lantern Hill Road).
- Right for 3.2 miles to crossroads and stop sign (Route 214, un-marked).
  After 2.5 miles, Lantern Hill Pond, with Lantern Hill behind it, is on your right. The ride turns right on Route 214, but to see the Indian museum go straight for 0.3 mile.
- Right (left if you visited the museum) for 0.3 mile to end (Route 2). You'll pass the main entrance to the casino on your left.
- Right for 2.2 miles to Rider Road on left, immediately after traffic light. Route 2 is busy with Foxwoods traffic, but there's a wide shoulder. After about 0.5 mile, stop for a view of the casino complex looming in the distance behind you.

- Left (*Caution* here—you may have to wait awhile for a break in the traffic) for 1.7 miles to end.
- Jog right and immediately left on Chester Main Road for 2 miles to end (Hangman Hill Road). The winery is on your right after 0.7 mile at top of steep part of hill, across from Arbor House Bed and Breakfast.
- Left for 1.6 miles to crossroads and stop sign (Route 49, Pendleton Hill Road).
- Straight for 1 mile to end (Denison Hill Road, unmarked).
- Right for 2.4 miles to second crossroads and stop sign, immediately after restaurant on left. Parking lot is on far left corner.

17 miles

- Follow first 7 directions of long ride, to Wyassup Road. Here the ride turns right, but it's worth turning left for 0.1 mile to the center of North Stonington. Turn into the parking lot on your right immediately after Main Street on your right to see the stream flowing behind the gristmill. Main Street is lined with handsome buildings.
- Right on Wyassup Road for 0.7 mile to Chester Main Road on right, just after Reuteman Road on right.
- Right for 2 miles to end (Hangman Hill Road). The winery is on your right after 0.7 mile at top of steep part of hill, across from Arbor House Bed and Breakfast.
- Follow last 3 directions of long ride.

Falls, where you'll pass a weathered gristmill beside a small dam.

The short ride continues a few miles west into the magnificent ridge-and-valley country of eastern Connecticut. Babcock Road, a narrow byway, winds past horse farms to a point just outside the gracious village center of North Stonington. It's worth detouring a few hundred yards to see the village, which contains a handsome stone school and library, a classic New England church, and sturdy wooden houses from the early 1800s. An old gristmill, complete with a rugged wooden millwheel and picturesque stream flowing behind it, adds to the charm of the hamlet.

Shortly after you turn east back toward Rhode Island, Chester Main Road climbs the toughest hill of the ride onto a high, open ridge with a full circle of sweeping views. Just before the top is the Kruger Main Farm Winery. Although it is not formally open to the public, someone will be glad to show you around, if available. You may wish to call beforehand (860–535–4650). A long, relaxing descent from the ridge rewards you for the climb. The rest of the route leads past dairy farms and fields of tall corn.

The long ride continues west through the village center of North Stonington to the entrance to the massive Foxwoods Casino, the largest Native American–owned gambling establishment in the country. You'll enjoy a relaxing ride along the shore of Long Pond about 2 miles before the casino. Just ahead is Lantern Hill Pond, with a dramatic view of rugged Lantern Hill rising behind it. Foxwoods is worth visiting for a bit of social observation (and good food) even if you have no interest in gambling. It includes a nine-story hotel, a striking museum of the history of the Mashantucket Pequot tribe in its own building, some high-tech video entertainment, some impressive Indian-themed sculpture, and a row of overpriced shops. You'll rejoin the short ride not far before the winery.

**Westerly–Watch Hill–
Ashaway**

Number of miles:	17 (32 with Ashaway extension)
Terrain:	Flat, with a couple of little hills. The long ride has one difficult climb.
Start:	Benny's, junction of Route 1 and Dunns Corner-Bradford Road, Westerly. It's about 4.5 miles southeast of the center of town.
Food:	Restaurant in downtown Westerly. Olympia Tea Room, Watch Hill, with old-fashioned, homey atmosphere—excellent place for a snack. Numerous snack bars along Misquamicut Beach in summer. McDonald's at end, on Route 1 just east of starting point.
Caution:	Unless you go early in the morning, it's best not to do this ride on summer weekends because of heavy beach traffic along the shore.

The southwestern corner of Rhode Island contains some of the most scenic bicycling in the state. Along the magnificent coastline are graceful old homes, resort hotels, and estates standing guard above the waves. Misquamicut Beach is one of the finest in the state. The Pawcatuck River, which forms the southern boundary between Rhode Island and Connecticut, widens from a picturesque millstream to a broad estuary lined with little coves. To the north are the rolling woods and farmlands typical of the southern third of the state, fondly known as South County.

The short ride comprises the area along the Pawcatuck River estuary and the ocean. At the beginning of the ride you pass north of Winnapaug Pond, one of the larger salt ponds in the state. Just after

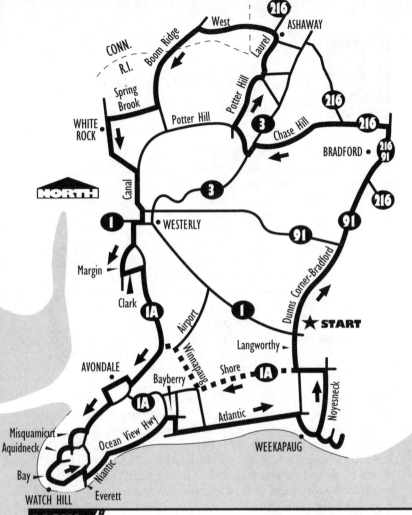

216 ASHAWAY

West

Boom Ridge

CONN.

R.I.

Spring Brook

Laurel

Potter Hill

WHITE ROCK

Potter Hill

Potter Hill

3

Chase Hill

216

216

BRADFORD •

216 91

Canal

3

216

1 • WESTERLY

91

91

Margin

Dunns Corner-Bradford

Clark

1A

Airport

1

Langworthy ►

★ **START**

AVONDALE

Winnapaug

Shore

1A

Bayberry

1A

Noyesneck

Atlantic ►

Misquamicut
Aquidneck

Ocean View Hwy

Niantic

WEEKAPAUG

Bay ►

WATCH HILL   Everett

NORTH

HOW to get there   From the north, head south on I–95 to exit 1 (Route 3). Bear right at end of ramp for about 5 miles to Route 78 (Westerly Bypass). Left (east) on bypass for 2.7 miles to Route 1. Left for 2.3 miles to Benny's on left, just after traffic light.

From the west, exit south from I–95 onto Route 2 (exit 92). Go 1.3 miles to Route 78 (Westerly Bypass). Bear right (east) on bypass for 5 miles to Route 1. Left for 2.3 miles to Benny's on left, just past traffic light.

- Left on Dunns Corner-Bradford Road, and just ahead cross Route 1 at traffic light. Go 0.6 mile to crossroads and stop sign (Route 1A, Shore Road). *Note:* Long ride turns right out of parking lot instead of left.
- Right for 2.5 miles to traffic light (Winnapaug Road).
- Right for 0.9 mile to where main road curves sharply left (sign indicates Watch Hill).
- Curve left for 0.2 mile to end (Route 1A, Watch Hill Road).
- Left for 1 mile to where main road curves sharply left, at grassy traffic island.
- Straight (don't curve left) and just ahead right at end. Go 0.2 mile to end (Pawcatuck River in front of you).
- Left for 1 mile to end (Watch Hill Road, unmarked).
- Right for 0.6 mile to Misquamicut Road on right.
- Right for 0.5 mile to fork where Sequan Road bears left.
- Bear right and just ahead turn right at crossroads (Aquidneck Avenue). Stay on main road for 0.2 mile to stop sign at bottom of hill (Bay Street).
- Bear right. Follow main road for 0.7 mile to Everett Avenue, a small crossroads shortly after huge wooden Ocean House on right. To visit Coast Guard station, turn right after 0.4 mile onto narrow lane. It's on the right just before you curve 90 degrees left, almost at top of hill. Please *walk* along the lane. It is a private road open to pedestrians only. It's 0.3 mile to the end of the lane.
- Jog right on Everett Avenue and immediately left on Niantic Avenue. Go 0.3 mile to stop sign.
- Straight for 1.4 miles to Bayberry Road on right. It's the first right after a long stretch with no roads on right.
- Right for 0.2 mile to crossroads (Maplewood Avenue).
- Right for 0.3 mile to end (Atlantic Avenue).
- Left for 3.1 miles to crossroads and stop sign immediately after small bridge.
- Right along ocean for 0.8 mile to dead-end sign.

- Backtrack along ocean for 0.2 mile to second fork (Noyesneck Road bears slightly right, main road curves left along water).
- Bear right for 1 mile to crossroads and stop sign (Shore Road, unmarked).
- Left for 0.5 mile to crossroads (Weekapaug Road on left, Langworthy Road on right).
- Right for 0.6 mile to Route 1. Benny's is on far right corner.

32 miles

- Right on Dunns Corner-Bradford Road for 2.1 miles to stop sign (Route 91 on left and straight).
- Straight for 2.6 miles to Route 216 North on left (sign says ASHAWAY).
- Left for 0.8 mile to where Route 216 curves right and Chase Hill Road bears slightly left (almost straight) up steep hill.
- Bear slightly left for 2.3 miles to end (Route 3, Main Street).
- Jog left and immediately right on Hiscox Road. Go 0.4 mile to first right (Potter Hill Road, unmarked), at stop sign.
- Right for 1 mile to road on left immediately after bridge. *Caution:* Watch for potholes on bridge.
- Turn left. Just ahead is a fork. Bear left along river for 0.8 mile to end (Route 216).
- Left for 100 yards to fork (main road bears right).
  Here the ride bears left, but if you bear right for 1.2 miles you'll come to an excellent truck-stop restaurant just after passing underneath I–95. *Caution:* Watch for bumps and potholes on this 1.2 mile segment.
- Bear left on West Street (turn right if you're coming from the restaurant) for 1.4 miles to end (Boom Bridge Road, unmarked).
- Left for 1.7 miles to Spring Brook Road on right. It comes up suddenly while you're going downhill.
- Right for 0.8 mile to end.
- Left for 0.8 mile to end (merge right on Canal Street).
- Bear right and stay on main road for 1 mile to end (Route 1), in downtown Westerly.

- Jog right and immediately left on Route 1A. (*Caution:* Watch for traffic.) After 0.1 mile, curve slightly right (sign says BEACHES). Go 0.4 mile to fork (Margin Street bears right along river).
- Bear right for 0.5 mile to Clark Street on left (dead end if you go straight).
- Left for 0.3 mile to end (Route 1A).
- Right for 2.7 miles to where the main road curves sharply left at grassy traffic island.
- Follow last 16 directions of short ride, beginning with "Straight (don't curve left) . . ."

---

you come to the river, you pass through the well-manicured water-front community of Avondale and then down to Watch Hill.

Watch Hill is an old, well-to-do resort town with smart shops, elegant waterfront homes, and rambling Victorian resort hotels. The nation's earliest operating carousel, built before 1871, is located here. A footpath leads out to Napatree Point, the westernmost point of land in the state. The point, which contained a row of cottages destroyed during the 1938 hurricane, has reverted to its natural state. At Watch Hill's extreme southern tip is the Watch Hill Coast Guard station, among the more spectacular places in Rhode Island. It offers nearly a 360-degree panorama of the Atlantic. A couple of miles to the east begins Misquamicut Beach, a narrow spit between the ocean and Winnapaug Pond. Just past Misquamicut you go through the graceful oceanfront community of Weekapaug, with handsome gabled and turreted homes perched on the rocky shoreline.

The long ride starts by heading north, away from the coast, through farms and woodland to the mill village of Bradford; here you cross the Pawcatuck River into Hopkinton. Turn west on Chase Hill Road, an idyllic lane that climbs sharply and then descends back into the valley. Parallel the river to Ashaway, passing two picturesque dams. This mill village, part of the town of Hopkinton, is known for its manufacture of fishing line.

From Ashaway, turn west and pedal through Connecticut for about 2 miles. Now the landscape changes, with broad fields, full of cows, sweeping up gentle hillsides. Cross the Pawcatuck back into Rhode Island and enter the mill village of White Rock, with its striking Victorian mill built in 1849. Pedal along the river through downtown Westerly and past the point where it widens into a tidal estuary. The railroad station, a stucco and brick building dating from 1912, is particularly attractive. It's on the left as you come into the downtown area, immediately after you go under the railroad bridge. Turn left on Railroad Avenue for 50 yards to see it. Continue on to join the short ride for the trip to Watch Hill and along the ocean.

Block Island

Number of miles:	16
Terrain:	Delightfully rolling, with lots of little ups and downs and a nice downhill ride at the end.
Start:	Ferry dock at Old Harbor, in the center of town. The ferries from Galilee, Providence, Newport, and New London, Connecticut, land here.
Food:	Grocery store and snack bar in town.
Caution:	Block Island has a unique hazard—mopeds, which are rented by the hundreds during the summer with no instruction on how to operate them safely. Mopeds frequently stop dead in the middle of the road without warning. I've also seen moped riders wobbling along with one arm full of parcels and overloaded wire baskets spilling their contents into the road.

Block Island offers 16 miles of some of the most delightful cycling and scenery in the state. The teardrop-shaped island, about 10 miles out to sea, is 5 miles long and 3 miles across at its widest point. The northern half is dominated by Great Salt Pond, which extends across the entire width of the island except for a narrow strip.

The Block Island landscape is unlike anything else in the state. The island is treeless, containing a unique scrubby, moorland vegetation which rises and falls in an endless series of small bubblelike hills and hollows. On the southeastern shore are the magnificent Mohegan Bluffs, rising over 100 feet nearly straight up from the sea and carved by erosion into jagged formations.

The boat from Galilee lands in town, a picturesque mixture of

rambling Victorian hotels and trim wooden homes. Just out of town is the fine public beach. From here head to the northern tip, where a dirt path leads nearly a mile to the North Lighthouse, standing in bleak, total isolation amidst an eerie landscape of sand dunes and sea. The lighthouse has been renovated into a maritime museum.

After returning toward town, circle the wide southern half of the island on roads winding through the moors, with views of the ocean around every curve. The architectural styles of the summer homes vary widely, from traditional cedar-shingled, peaked-roof cottages to bold ultramodern structures with sharp angles that seem even sharper against the stark, treeless landscape. You'll pass Rodman's Hollow, a bowl-shaped ravine with hiking trails. Near the end of the ride, from the top of Mohegan Bluffs, you'll gaze in wonder at one of the most spectacular views in Rhode Island.

Just past the Bluffs is Southeast Lighthouse, a graceful brick landmark built in 1873. It contains a museum of lighthouse history, open during the summer. Because the cliffs behind the building are eroding, it was moved 200 feet inland in 1993 to prevent it from toppling into the sea.

A trip to Block Island should be an unhurried, leisurely experience. Take an early boat and spend the day or even a weekend poking around the numerous dirt roads leading down to the ocean or to the Coast Guard Station on Great Salt Pond. You can easily spend a couple of hours exploring Mohegan Bluffs alone. When you get back to town, browse through the colorful gift and antiques shops or relax at the beach. If it's a warm, clear day, treat yourself to the four-hour ferry trip from Providence, which follows the entire length of Narragansett Bay and stops at Newport before continuing on to Block Island. You'll have less time to explore the island unless you stay overnight, but the delightful trip along the bay will more than make up for it. If you stay overnight, be sure to make reservations in advance. Camping is not permitted.

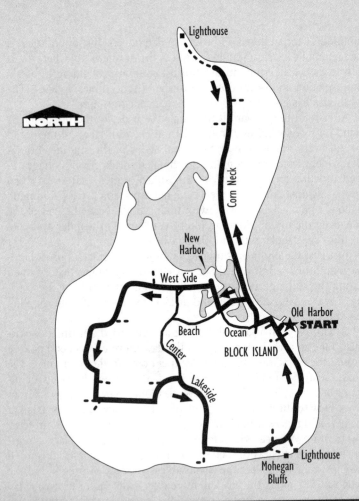

NORTH

Lighthouse

Corn Neck

New Harbor

West Side

Old Harbor
★ START

Beach

Ocean

Center

BLOCK ISLAND

Lakeside

Lighthouse

Mohegan Bluffs

HOW to get there
To get to Galilee, exit south from Route 1 onto Route 108. Go about 4 miles to the road to Galilee on right. Follow this road to end and turn left. Ferry dock is just ahead. The Providence ferry dock is on India Street at the head of the harbor. From I–195, take the Gano Street exit and turn left at the end of the exit ramp. Go to end, just ahead, and turn right on India Street. The dock is 0.25 mile ahead on left. For schedules, call the Block Island Boat, 401–783–4613, or AAA.

**DIREC-
TIONS
for the ride**

- Right at end of dock entrance. Just ahead road turns 90 degrees left. Go 0.1 mile to crossroads and stop sign (Corn Neck Road, unmarked, on right).
- Right for 3.7 miles to end. From here a dirt path leads 0.7 mile to North Lighthouse and another 0.3 mile to Sandy Point, the extreme tip.
- Backtrack for 3.3 miles to first main road on right, Beach Avenue (unmarked). It crosses small bridge.
- Right for 0.4 mile to first right, at stop sign (Ocean Avenue, unmarked).
- Right for 0.3 mile to West Side Road (unmarked) on left. New Harbor dock is straight ahead.
- Left for 0.2 mile to fork.
- Bear right for 3.8 miles to end (merge right at stop sign).
- Bear right on Lakeside Drive (unmarked). After 1 mile the main road curves 90 degrees left and a dirt road bears right. Curve left for 0.9 mile to a dirt turnoff that bears to the right. From the turnoff a footpath leads 50 yards to Mohegan Bluffs. It's shortly before the redbrick Southeast Lighthouse.
- Continue on main road for 0.25 mile to another footpath on right that leads to bicycle racks (sign says EDWARD S. PAYNE OVERLOOK). The main viewing area for the bluffs is 100 yards beyond the racks. A stairway leads down to the beach.
- Continue 1.6 miles to crossroads and stop sign at bottom of hill. You'll pass Southeast Lighthouse at the beginning.
- Bear left to dock, just ahead on right.

East Providence–Riverside

Number of miles:	15
Terrain:	Gently rolling, with two hills.
Start:	East Providence Cycle, 414 Warren Avenue, East Providence.
Food:	Numerous snack bars and grocery stores along route. Excellent deli and ice cream shop in Riverside Square next to bike path.
Facilities:	Rest rooms at Looff Carousel.

CAUTION:

The East Bay Bicycle Path is very heavily used in good weather by both cyclists and noncyclists. Please read *Caution* in the "Bikeways" section of the introduction.

Here is a tour of the southern half of East Providence, a residential community directly across the uppermost part of Narragansett Bay from Providence. Although the region is suburban, its long frontage on the bay provides pleasant and scenic bicycling on a beautiful section of the East Bay Bicycle Path.

The ride starts about a mile inland from the Providence River, which is actually the relatively narrow northern arm of Narragansett Bay. Head inland briefly through Kent Heights, a pleasant residential area on a high ridge overlooking the rest of East Providence, passing the big mushroom-shaped water tower. A mile ahead, bike past a forest of gasoline and oil tanks at a distribution facility of the Mobil Oil Corporation. The oil arrives by tanker at the dock 2 miles away; you'll pass it later on the bike path.

Beyond the Mobil facility, head south and west through Riverside, the residential southern quarter of East Providence. Just before you come to the bay, you'll see the former grounds of Crescent Park, one of New England's leading amusement parks during the early 1900s. On the grounds is a round, gaily painted building containing a masterpiece of folk art, an ornately carved sixty-two-horse carousel constructed in 1895 by Charles Looff, a noted woodcarver. When the park went out of business in 1975, the land reverted to the city, which sold it several years later to a developer who built apartments next to the carousel. An enraged citizenry, fearful that the carousel would be demolished, sued to have it brought back under city ownership and won their suit. The carousel is still in operating condition and is open during the warmer half of the year. Opposite the carousel is a small park with a superb view of the bay.

Now loop around residential Bullocks Point, a narrow peninsula forming the southern tip of East Providence. Pass the carousel again and just ahead get onto the East Bay Bicycle Path, which you will follow for over 4 miles almost to the end of the ride. The bike path, which is the scenic highlight of the ride, hugs the shore of Narragansett Bay for most of this section. Formerly a Providence & Worcester Railroad track, the path is flat except for a short, steep hill toward the end.

At the beginning the path follows Bullocks Cove, a small inlet of the bay. A mile ahead is Riverside Square, where you can stop at a good ice cream shop or deli next to the path. Soon the path converges with the shore of the bay, where you'll see an old, picturesque lighthouse perched on a tiny island a few hundred feet offshore. After a mile go past the Squantum Association, an exclusive private club, and then ride along a causeway with Watchemoket Cove on your right and the bay on your left. Just ahead you ascend Fort Hill, a low ridge with dramatic views of downtown Providence across the river. At the end of the bike path, it's only a mile back to the starting point. As you turn onto Warren Avenue, notice the Comedy Connection on the right, a former bank with an enormous duck protruding from the roof.

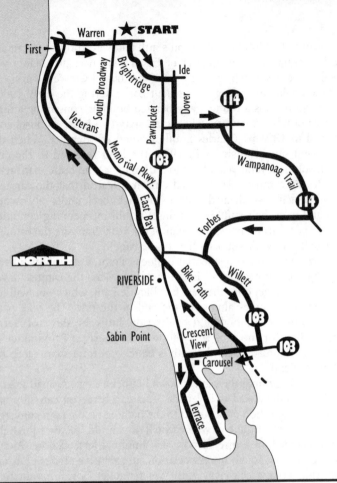

First · Warren · ★ START
South Broadway
Brightridge
Ide
Veterans
Pawtucket
Dover
114
Memorial Pkwy.
103
Wampanoag Trail
East Bay
114
Forbes
NORTH
RIVERSIDE
Bike Path
Willett
Sabin Point
103
Crescent View
103
Carousel
Terrace

HOW to get there From I–95, head east on I–195 to exit 6 (sign says BROADWAY). Turn right, and the shop is the first building on your right. If you're heading west on I–195, take exit 6 (sign says EAST PROVIDENCE). Turn left, go to traffic light at Warren Avenue; turn left for 0.2 mile to store on left.

By bike from Providence, head east on Waterman Street, cross bridge over Seekonk River, and take first exit. Just ahead road curves 90 degrees left. Take second right on Walnut Street for 0.6 mile to end (Warren Avenue), shortly after you cross Taunton Avenue. Left for 0.8 mile to store on left.

- Left on Warren Avenue for 0.1 mile to second right (Brightridge Avenue).
- Right for 0.6 mile to end (Pawtucket Avenue).
- Jog left and immediately right on Ide Avenue. Go 1 block to crossroads and stop sign (Dover Avenue).

- Right for 0.5 mile to busy crossroads and stop sign (Wampanoag Trail).
- Left for 0.5 mile to Route 114 South on right (sign says BARRINGTON, BRISTOL). Route 114 is a busy highway, but there's a wide shoulder.
- Right for 1.8 miles to Forbes Street on right, after access road to Mobil distribution facility.
- Right for 1.4 miles to end (Willett Avenue, unmarked).
- Left for 1.3 miles to end (Crescent View Avenue; sign points left to Barrington and right to Riverside).
- Right for 0.7 mile to end (Bullocks Point Avenue, unmarked). Carousel on left at corner. (After 0.25 mile you'll cross the East Bay Bike Path, which leads about 9 miles on your left to Bristol).
- Left 0.2 mile to fork, at stop sign.
- Turn right on Terrace Avenue (the street sign is visible after the turn). Another sign may say DEAD END, but it's not. After 0.7 mile, road turns 90 degrees left, then 90 degrees left again just ahead onto Riverside Drive. Continue for 0.9 mile to Crescent View Avenue on right, just past carousel.
- Right for 0.4 mile to bike path, which crosses road at blinking light.
- Left on bike path for 4.4 miles to end (First Street, unmarked). *Caution:* End of bike path is at bottom of steep hill. Also, the path is very heavily used in good weather. Please read *Caution* in the "Bikeways" section of the introduction.
- Left on First Street for 0.2 mile to end (Warren Avenue).
- Right for 0.9 mile to store on left, shortly after the traffic light at Broadway. *Caution* crossing Broadway—busy intersection.

Seekonk–Attleboro–Mansfield–Norton

Number of miles:	16 (27 with Mansfield–Norton extension, 10 with shortcut)
Terrain:	Gently rolling.
Start:	Ro-Jack's Fresh Marketplace, Route 152 in Seekonk, Massachusetts, about 5 miles south of the center of Attleboro.
Food:	Bliss Brothers Dairy, Route 118 opposite Bishop Street, Attleboro. Country store and grocery in West Mansfield. Grocery and restaurant at junction of Route 118 and Tremont Street in Rehoboth.
Facilities:	Rest rooms at La Salette Shrine, Attleboro.

Northeast of Providence, just across the Massachusetts state line, is a semi-rural, semi-suburban region that is a pleasure for bicycling. Although close to both the city and the commuter rail line to Boston, the area is not heavily built-up, and it abounds with lightly-traveled secondary roads that weave past well-kept houses interspersed with small fields and woodlots. This is one of the flattest rides in the book, and you'll enjoy some long, smooth sections without a lot of turns.

The ride starts from the northern edge of Seekonk and soon crosses into Attleboro on Oak Hill Avenue, a popular road for cycling that passes a traditional red schoolhouse. After turning north on Route 118, you'll pass La Salette Shrine, a perfect spot for quiet contemplation complete with gardens, statuary, Stations of the Cross, and a flight of twenty-eight stone steps ascending to an enormous crucifix. La Salette is best known for its dazzling display of lights during the Christmas season; it's among the largest in the country. After feeding your soul, just ahead you may feed your body at Bliss Brothers Dairy, an excellent spot for ice cream and snacks.

The rest of the short ride is more rural as it heads east and then south along the sparsely-populated eastern edge of Attleboro into the northern part of Rehoboth. You'll go past a small farm with alpacas and miniature donkeys on Harvey Road; it will be on your left at the end. Finish the ride along Tremont Street (which becomes Woodlawn Avenue in Seekonk), another long, smooth secondary road that is a favorite with local bicyclists.

The long ride continues farther north into Mansfield and Norton, two pleasant towns on the southern fringe of the Boston metropolitan area. Mansfield is suburban in the affluent sense of the word, with many impressive new homes on one- and two-acre wooded lots. You'll pass a millpond opposite a wooden factory built in 1853, and just ahead enter the handsome village of West Mansfield, a former stop on the railroad between Providence and Boston. The old train station stands next to a combined country store and gift shop that is tasteful rather than tacky. Soon you'll enter Norton, which is more rural than Mansfield. Norton is best known for the graceful campus of Wheaton College, which is 2 miles east of the ride on Route 123. Maple Street winds past small farms and rejoins the short ride about a mile before it enters Rehoboth.

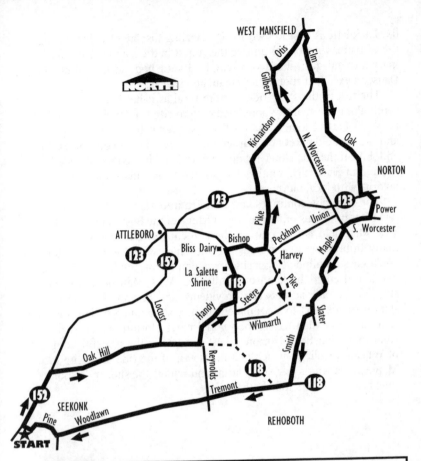

NORTH

WEST MANSFIELD

Otis
Elm
Gilbert
Richardson
N. Worcester
Oak

NORTON

123
Pike
Peckham
Union
123
Power
S. Worcester

ATTLEBORO
123
Bishop
Harvey
Maple
152
Bliss Dairy
La Salette Shrine
118
Steere
Pike
Slater
Handy
Wilmarth
Locust
Reynolds
Smith
118
Oak Hill
Tremont
118
152
SEEKONK
Woodlawn
REHOBOTH
Pine
START

HOW to get there

From I–95, exit south onto Route 1A, Newport Avenue (exit 2A). Go 1 mile to third traffic light (Central Avenue). Left for 1 mile to end (Route 152). Turn right, and supermarket is just ahead on left.

From I–195, exit north onto Route 114A (exit 1). After 1 mile Route 114A bears left, but go straight for about 2 miles to end (Route 152). Right for 3.3 miles to supermarket on right.

From the East Side of Providence (and by bike from Providence), head east on Waterman Street, cross bridge over Seekonk River, and take second exit. Bear right at end of ramp for 0.3 mile to traffic light (North Broadway). Left for 5 miles to supermarket on right.

- Right on Route 152 for 1 mile to Oak Hill Avenue on right.
- Right for 3 miles to Handy Street on left, immediately before Reynolds Street on right.
  It comes up suddenly while you're curving left down a short hill. Here the 10-mile ride goes straight.

- Left for 1 mile to end (Route 118), at top of short, steep hill. Notice old wooden school on right at the beginning.
- Left for 1.1 miles to Bishop Street on right, at blinking light. Bliss Brothers Dairy is on your left at the intersection. You'll pass La Salette Shrine on your left.
- Right for 0.8 mile to end (Pike Avenue). Here the 16-mile ride turns right.
- Left for 1.2 miles to end (Route 123, Pleasant Street).
- Left for 0.25 mile to Richardson Avenue on right.
- Right for 1.8 miles to crossroads and stop sign (North Worcester Street).
- Left for 1 mile to Otis Street on right.
- Right for 1.1 miles to crossroads and stop sign, in West Mansfield.
- Right for 1.1. miles to Oak Street on left, shortly after grocery on left.
- Left for 3 miles to end (Route 123).
- Left for 0.2 mile to Power Street on right.
- Right and just ahead right again (still Power Street) for 0.6 mile to end (South Worcester Street).
  There's an attractive white church on your left at the end.
- Right for 0.5 mile to crossroads and stop sign (South Worcester Street on right, John B. Scott Boulevard on left).
- Left for 0.1 mile to Maple Street Extension on right. *Caution:* Diagonal railroad tracks.
- Right and just ahead left at stop sign. Go 2 miles to Smith Street on right, shortly after Wilmarth Street on right.
- Right for 1.5 miles to end (Route 118).
- Right for 0.4 mile to fork where Route 118 bears right and Tremont Street bears left.

- Bear left for 4 miles to end (Pine Street, unmarked).
- Right for almost 0.5 mile to Plainfield Street on left, just before traffic light at Route 152.
- Left for 0.1 mile to end, passing behind the supermarket from which you started. *Caution:* Speed bump as you approach supermarket.

16 miles

- Follow first 5 directions of long ride, to Pike Avenue.
- Right for 0.1 mile to fork (Harvey Road bears left).
- Bear left for 0.2 mile to end (Pike Avenue again, unmarked). There's a small farm with alpacas and miniature donkeys on your left at the end.
- Left for 0.4 mile to fork (Steere Street bears right, Pike Avenue bears left).
- Bear left for 0.6 mile to end (Wilmarth Street).
- Left for 0.5 mile to end (Slater Street).
- Right for 0.2 mile to Smith Street on right.
- Follow last 5 directions of long ride.

10 miles

- Follow first 2 directions of long ride, to Handy Street.
- Straight for 0.5 mile to Route 118 (unmarked), at stop sign.
- Right for 0.8 mile to Tremont Street, which turns sharply right at traffic island. Route 118 bears left at the intersection.
- Sharp right for 4 miles to end (Pine Street, unmarked).
- Follow last 2 directions of long ride.

Seekonk–Rehoboth
Northern Ride

Number of miles:	13 (26 with Rehoboth extension, 18 with short-cut)
Terrain:	Gently rolling, with two hills. The 26-mile ride has two additional short, steep hills.
Start:	Vacant shopping center at the northeast corner of Routes 44 and 114A, Seekonk, Massachusetts.
Food:	None on the short ride. Grocery store at corner of Fairview Avenue and Route 118. Country store at corner of County and Reservoir Streets. Burger King and McDonald's on Route 44, 1 mile west of starting point.

The two towns of Seekonk and Rehoboth, just east of Providence across the Massachusetts state line, offer some of the finest cycling in the entire Rhode Island–nearby Massachusetts area. The region is fairly flat, unusually rural considering how close it is to the city, and protected by strict zoning laws that are preventing the onslaught of suburbanization. An extensive network of well-paved, narrow country lanes winds past large farms, a couple of ponds, and rustic, weathered old barns and farmhouses. The center of Rehoboth is a gem, with a perfect little dam and millpond, a fine small church, and the graceful brick Goff Memorial building, which holds the town library.

The proximity of the Seekonk–Rehoboth region to Providence makes it very easy to reach by bicycle, especially from the city's East Side. From the bridge at the end of Waterman Street that connects Providence and East Providence, it is only 3 or 4 miles to the start of this ride and the two following ones.

The ride starts from the Seekonk–East Providence line and within

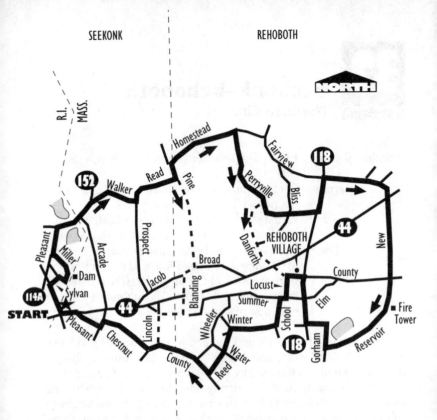

HOW to get there

From I–95, exit east onto I–195 for about 2 miles to Taunton Avenue exit (Route 44). Follow Route 44 for about 2 miles to shopping center on left, just past Route 114A.

From the east, exit north from I–195 onto Route 114A (exit 1). Go 1.7 miles to Route 44. Shopping center is on far right corner.

By bike from Providence, head east on Waterman Street, cross bridge, and take second exit. Bear right at end of ramp for 0.3 mile to traffic light (North Broadway). Left for 0.2 mile to traffic light. Right on Centre Street for 0.5 mile to end (Pawtucket Avenue). Left for 0.3 mile to traffic light. Right on Route 114A (Pleasant Street) for 0.6 mile to shopping center on left.

DIRECTIONS
for the ride

26 miles

- Right on Route 114A for 0.5 mile to Sylvan Road on right, just after Carriage Lane on right.
- Right and just ahead right again (still Sylvan Road) for 1 block to end (Hood Avenue).
- Right for 0.3 mile to crossroads (Pleasant Street). The street makes 2 elbow bends to the left. At the second bend there's a dam on your right. The Turner Reservoir is above the dam and the Ten Mile River flows below it.
- Right for 0.4 mile to wide crossroads and stop sign (Route 152). *Caution:* The first two blocks are very bumpy.
- Right for 1.1 miles to Walker Street, which bears right. You'll cross the Turner Reservoir at the beginning.
- Bear right for 1 mile to end (Prospect Street). You'll pass the athletic fields of the Wheeler School, a girls' preparatory school whose main campus is on the East Side of Providence.
- Left for 1.5 miles to end (Pine Street, unmarked), at top of hill. Here the 13-mile ride turns right and the 18-mile ride turns left.
- Left and just ahead right on Homestead Avenue for 1.9 miles to Perryville Road on right. It's 0.5 mile after a small crossroads.
- Right for 1.2 miles to Danforth Street on right. Here the 18-mile ride turns right and the 26-mile ride goes straight.
  There's a small pond and dam on your right immediately before the intersection.
- Straight for 1.2 miles to end (Anawan Street, Route 118).
- Left for 0.7 mile to crossroads (Fairview Avenue). There's a grocery on the far left corner.
- Right for 1.5 miles to fork at top of second hill (main road bears right).
- Bear right for 0.3 mile to traffic light (Route 44).
- Go straight for 1.8 miles to crossroads and stop sign (County Street, unmarked). Country store on far left corner.
- Straight for 2.1 miles to end (Gorham Street). Fire tower on left after 0.5 mile; you may go up if it's open.
- Right for 1.1 miles to crossroads and stop sign (Route 118).

- Right for 0.8 mile to second crossroads (County Street), at blinking light.
- Left for 0.3 mile to stop sign (merge left on Bay State Road).
- Bear left for 0.2 mile to Locust Avenue on left, in Rehoboth Village.
- Left for 0.5 mile to end.
- Right and just ahead left on School Street. Go 0.9 mile to Winter Street on right.
- Right for 1.1 miles to end, where Lake Street turns left and also bears right.
- Left for 0.2 mile to fork (Reed Street bears left).
- Bear left for 0.8 mile to end (Providence Street, unmarked). You'll pass the dam at Shad Factory Pond on your right.
- Right for 1.4 miles to Chestnut Street on right, while going uphill.
- Right for 1.5 miles to end (Arcade Avenue, unmarked).
- Left and just ahead right on Pleasant Street for 0.4 mile to Route 44, at stop sign.
- Bear left (*Caution*) for 0.1 mile to shopping center on right.

13 miles

- Follow first 7 directions of 26-mile ride to Pine Street.
- Right for 2.2 miles to end (Broad Street).
- Right for 0.5 mile to Blanding Road on left.
- Left for 0.4 mile to crossroads and stop sign (Route 44, Winthrop Street).
- Go straight (*Caution*) for 0.4 mile to end.
- Right for 0.6 mile to crossroads and stop sign at top of hill (Lincoln Street).
- Left for 1.1 miles to crossroads and stop sign (County Street).
- Right for 0.2 mile to Chestnut Street on right.
- Follow last 3 directions of 26-mile ride.

18 miles

- Follow first 9 directions of 26-mile ride, to Danforth Street on right.

- Turn right and stay on main road for 1.6 miles to crossroads and stop sign (Route 44).
- Right for 0.6 mile to Locust Avenue on right, in Rehoboth Village.
- Right for 0.5 mile to end.
- Follow last 8 directions of 26-mile ride, beginning with "Right and just ahead left on School Street . . ."

---

a mile passes a fine dam at the southern end of the Turner Reservoir. Just ahead you'll cross the reservoir along a causeway and proceed onto small roads that lead into the more rural, eastern half of Seekonk. You'll climb gradually through farmland to the top of a hill at the Rehoboth town line. If you take the short ride, you'll enjoy a relaxing descent down the far side of the hill on Pine Street. The route continues south across Route 44, the busy east-west road that slashes across the two towns on its way to Taunton. Heading west back into Seekonk, you go through a more open area with some large farms and two expanses of town-owned conservation land.

The long ride heads farther east along winding, wooded lanes to Route 118, the main north-south road through Rehoboth, passing a small millpond with a picturesque little dam. Beyond this road the countryside is even more rural. You pass a horse farm and a fire tower that is sometimes open during the warmer half of the year, and then descend to the unspoiled Warren Upper Reservoir. After 2 miles you'll pedal into Rehoboth Village, where the small green is a pleasant spot for a rest. Just ahead is the Goff Memorial and the Carpenter Museum, which contains exhibits of local history and rural artifacts. The return trip brings you along delightful back roads through a harmonious mixture of forests and open fields, passing well-maintained farmhouses and grazing animals. The dam at Shad Factory Pond is a delightful spot. You rejoin the short ride just after you cross the Seekonk line.

The 18-mile ride stays west of Route 118, taking a direct route from the small millpond to Rehoboth Village.

Seekonk–Rehoboth
Southern Ride

Number of miles:	20 (12 with Palmer River Section only; 15 with Rehoboth Village section only)
Terrain:	Gently rolling, with a few short hills.
Start:	Briarwood Plaza, corner of County and Olney Streets, Seekonk, Massachusetts.
Food:	None on the route. Bakery and pizza at end.

The terrain and landscape of this ride through Seekonk and Rehoboth are similar to that of the northern ride, with little narrow roads winding past farms with weathered barns and stone walls. Of the three Seekonk–Rehoboth rides, this one passes through the most open farmland.

The ride starts by heading east across Seekonk on County Street, which quickly leads you into the countryside. After a mile you cross the Rehoboth town line and turn onto Reed Street, which descends a gentle grade to the picturesque Shad Factory Dam. The Palmer River begins here, flowing south for 6 or 7 miles until it enters Narragansett Bay between Barrington and Warren. Soon you'll head north through forests and small pastures on School Street, the kind of lane that seems to have been laid out with bicycling in mind.

Locust Street brings you into classic Rehoboth Village, passing the Carpenter Museum, which contains exhibits of local history and rural artifacts. In the village you'll see a traditional white church, followed by a lovely little dam on your right and the gracious Goff Memorial, a town building that includes the public library. A small green just ahead is a good spot for a rest or picnic lunch.

The ride now turns south along Chestnut Street, another narrow lane that runs through the most wooded section of the route. You'll

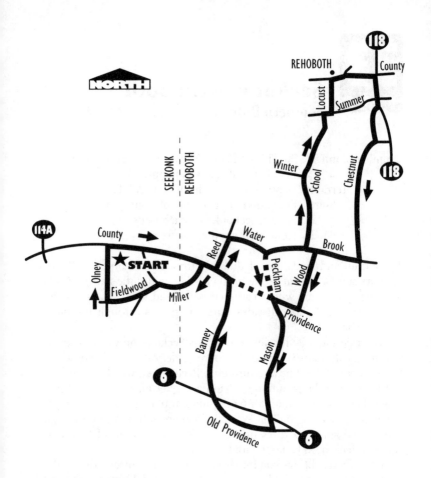

Exit north from I–195 onto Route 114A for 0.7 mile to traffic light. Right on County Street for 1 mile to plaza on right.

By bike from Providence, head east on Waterman Street, cross bridge, and take first exit. Just ahead, road curves 90 degrees left onto Waterman Avenue. Go 0.6 mile to end, at second traffic light. Left for 1.8 miles to end, staying on Waterman Avenue. Left for 0.2 mile to traffic light (Route 114A). Straight for 1 mile to plaza on right.

DIREC-TIONS for the ride

20 miles

- Right on County Street for 2.1 miles to Reed Street on left. It's 0.4 mile after Miller Street on right. There's a short, steep hill at the beginning.
- Left for 0.6 mile to crossroads and stop sign (Water Street).
- Right for 0.5 mile to fork. Here the 12-mile ride bears right.
- Bear left for 0.6 mile to School Street on left, while climbing short hill.
- Left for 1.7 miles to end, staying on main road. (Winter Street turns left after 0.9 mile, but curve right on main road.)
- Right and just ahead left on Locust Street for 0.5 mile to end, in Rehoboth Village.
- Right for 0.2 mile to fork (Bay State Road bears left, County Street bears right).
- Bear right for 0.3 mile to stop sign and blinking light (Route 118).
- Right for 0.3 mile to second right (Chestnut Street).
- Right for almost 0.6 mile to fork where one road turns left and the other bears right.
- Bear right (still Chestnut Street, unmarked) for 1.7 miles to crossroads (Brook Street).
- Right for 0.7 mile to Wood Street on left.
- Left for 0.8 mile to end (Providence Street, unmarked).
- Right for 0.4 mile to Mason Street on left (sharp left), at traffic island. Here the 15-mile ride goes straight.
- Sharp left for 2.1 miles to Route 6, at stop sign.
  At this point the ride goes straight and then right to a bridge that is under construction. If a sign indicates that the bridge is closed, turn right (west) on Route 6 for 0.8 mile to Barney Avenue, which bears right. Bear right for 1.9 mile to end. Resume 4 directions ahead, beginning "Left for 0.5 mile . . ."
- Cross Route 6 diagonally (*Caution* here). Go 0.1 mile to end (Old Providence Road).
- Right for 1 mile to Route 6, at stop sign.
- Cross Route 6 diagonally onto Barney Avenue (*Caution* again). Go 1.9 miles to end (Providence Street, unmarked).

- Left for 0.5 mile to Miller Street on left.
- Left for 0.9 mile to fork (Bradley Street, unmarked, bears right).
- Bear left for 0.5 mile to fork (Fieldwood Avenue goes straight).
- Straight (don't bear left) for 0.4 mile to crossroads and stop sign (Olney Street on right).
- Right for 1 mile to parking lot on right.

12 miles

- Follow first 3 directions of long ride, to fork.
- Bear right for 0.5 mile to diagonal crossroads (Providence Street, unmarked).
- Follow last 9 directions of long ride, going straight on Mason Street instead of turning sharp left.

15 miles

- Follow first 14 directions of long ride, to Mason Street on left.
- Straight for 1.1 miles to Miller Street on left. It's almost 0.4 mile after Reed Street on right.
- Follow last 4 directions of long ride.

---

zip down a little hill on Brook Street and then continue south on Mason Street, an idyllic byway passing broad, prosperous farms along the Palmer River. Cross the river at the point where it begins to widen into a tidal estuary. The aging bridge is currently blocked off to traffic, but you can detour a short distance to the north to Route 6. After crossing the river, the route heads north along the opposite bank, traversing more prime farmland full of cows and horses. The last 3 miles of the ride bring you past a few more large farms and a residential area.

Because the route is shaped somewhat like a figure-eight, there are two logical options for a shorter ride: You can omit the northern loop (which includes Rehoboth Village) and head directly to the roads along the Palmer River, shortening the distance to 12 miles; or you can visit Rehoboth Village but then omit the Palmer River section toward the end, shortening the ride to 15 miles.

34

Seekonk–Rehoboth
One More Time

Number of miles: 15 (25 with southern extension)

Terrain: Gently rolling, with one hill. The long ride has an additional hill.

Start: Seekonk High School, corner of Arcade Avenue and Ledge Road in Seekonk, 0.7 mile north of Route 44.

Food: None on short ride. Country store at corner of County and Reservoir Streets. Country store at corner of Plain Street and Route 118. Burger King and McDonald's on Route 44, 1.5 miles west of starting point.

The Seekonk–Rehoboth area is so ideal for bicycling and so accessible to Providence (twenty minutes by bike from the East Side), that it is worth including one more ride through the two towns. We'll explore the same general area covered by the southern ride but pedal along different roads for most of the route. The terrain is similar to that of the other two rides—pleasantly rolling, with an occasional hill for variety.

From Seekonk you bike past gentleman farms and large, gracious homes and then cross into Rehoboth. Here you head to Rehoboth Village, the tiny center of town, through a pastoral landscape of gently rolling farmland. The return to Seekonk leads through more of this landscape. The long ride heads farther east and south through an even more rural area. You pass Francis Farm, a popular spot for clambakes, and then pass a fire tower that is sometimes open. Just ahead you'll descend briskly to the Warren Upper Reservoir. After a few miles you pass Shad Factory Pond, a small millpond with a nice dam. From here it is a short ride back to the start.

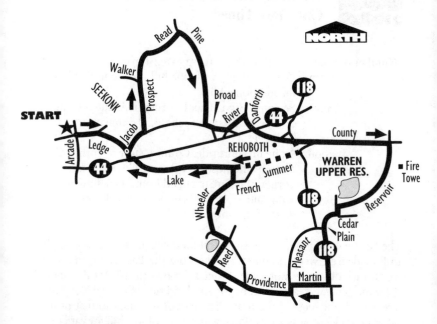

NORTH

START

SEEKONK

Read · Pine

Walker

Prospect

Broad

River

Danforth

118

44

Jacob

Arcade

Ledge

44

REHOBOTH •

County

Summer

WARREN
UPPER RES.

■ Fire
Towe

Lake

French

118

Reservoir

Wheeler

118

Cedar
Plain

Reed

Pleasant

118

Providence

Martin

HOW to get there From I–95, exit east onto I–195 for about 2 miles to exit 4 (Route 44, Taunton Avenue). Follow Route 44 almost 3 miles to Arcade Avenue, at traffic light. Left for 0.7 mile to school on left.

From the east, exit north from I–195 onto Route 114A (exit 1). After 1 mile Route 114A bears left, but go straight for 0.8 mile to traffic light (Route 44). Straight for 0.7 mile to school on left.

By bike from Providence, follow "How to get there" for Ride 32 to traffic light at Route 114A (Pleasant Street). Right for 0.3 mile to Ledge Road on left. Left for 0.6 mile to school on left.

- Left on Ledge Road for 0.1 mile to crossroads and stop sign (Arcade Avenue). *Caution:* Speed bump as you leave parking lot.
- Straight for 0.3 mile to fork (Greenwood Avenue bears left.)
- Bear right (still Ledge Road). Stay on main road for 0.9 mile to end (Jacob Street, unmarked). Don't bear right on Hope Street after 0.2 mile.
- Sharp left for 0.4 mile to Prospect Street on left.
- Left for 1.4 miles to fork (main road bears right).
- Bear right (still Prospect Street) and stay on main road for 1.5 miles to end (Pine Street, unmarked).
- Right for 2.2 miles to end (Broad Street).
- Left for 0.3 mile to fork (main road bears slightly left).
- Bear left for 0.3 mile to crossroads and stop sign (River Street).
- Bear left down a little hill for 0.7 mile to end (Danforth Street).
- Right for 0.3 mile to crossroads and stop sign (Route 44).
- Straight (*Caution*) for 0.8 mile to fork just past Rehoboth Village (Bay State Road bears left, County Street bears right).
- Bear right for 0.3 mile to blinking light (Route 118). Here the short ride turns right.
- Straight for 2.2 miles to crossroads and stop sign at top of hill. Country store on far right corner.
- Right for 2 miles to end (Gorham Street).
- Left for 0.2 mile to end (Cedar Street on left, Plain Street on right).
- Right for 0.6 mile to stop sign (Route 118).
- Bear slightly left onto Route 118 South. Go 1.2 miles to crossroads (Martin Street).
- Right for 1 mile to end (Pleasant Street, unmarked).
- Left and just ahead right on Providence Street. Go 2.1 miles to Reed Street on right. It's just after Barney Avenue on left.
- Right for 0.6 mile to crossroads and stop sign (Water Street).
- Left for 0.3 mile to yield sign at bottom of hill (Wheeler Street bears right).
- Bear right for 1.1 miles to yield sign where French Street bears

right and the main road bears left.

- Bear left for 0.3 mile to end (Summer Street, unmarked).
- Turn left and stay on main road for 2 miles to end, at second stop sign (merge left on Route 44).
- Bear left (*Caution* here) for 50 yards to Jacob Street on right.
- Turn right and just ahead bear left on Ledge Road. Go 1.2 miles to crossroads and stop sign (Arcade Avenue, unmarked).
- Straight for 0.1 mile to school entrance on right. *Caution:* Speed bump at entrance.

15 miles

- Follow first 13 directions of long ride, to Route 118.
- Right for 0.3 mile to crossroads (Elm Street on left, Summer Street on right).
- Turn right. Stay on the main road for 1.5 miles to fork where French Street bears left and the main road bears slightly right. It's shortly after you climb a steep little hill.
- Bear right and stay on main road for 2.3 miles to end, at second stop sign (merge left on Route 44).
- Follow last 3 directions of long ride.

Swansea–Somerset– Dighton–Rehoboth

Number of miles:	17 (30 with Rehoboth extension, 13 with short-cut)
Terrain:	Gently rolling, with one moderate hill and one tough one. The 13-mile ride avoids the tough hill.
Start:	McDonald's, Route 6, Swansea, Massachusetts.
Food:	None on 13-mile ride. Country store in Dighton. Restaurant at junction of Old Fall River Road and Route 6, Swansea (30-mile ride). McDonald's at end.

This ride takes you through the gently rolling countryside along the west bank of the lower Taunton River, the major river in the south-eastern part of Massachusetts. The route parallels the river for several miles and then returns along the ridge rising just inland from the west bank. The long ride heads farther west into farm country and then finishes with a relaxing ride along Mount Hope Bay, the broad estuary at the mouth of the river.

Start from Swansea, a pleasant rural community midway between Providence and Fall River and just far enough from either to have so far avoided suburban development.

From Swansea you traverse a low ridge into Somerset, which lies along the Taunton River across from Fall River. Most of Somerset is suburban, but you bike through the older and less-developed north-ern portion of town. Follow the river on a narrow street lined with fas-cinating old buildings and then continue to the center of Dighton, another attractive riverfront town extending westward into gently rolling farm country.

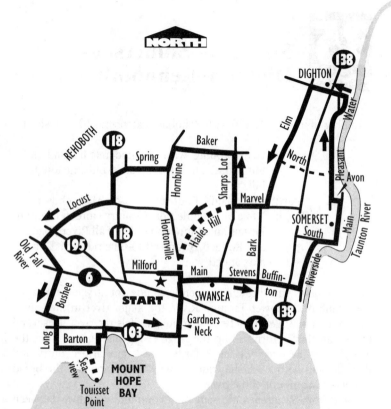

NORTH

REHOBOTH

118

Spring

Baker

Hornbine

Sharps Lot

Locust

118

Hortonville

Hailes Hill

Marvel

195

Old Fall River

Milford

★ START

Bushee

Main

Stevens

Bark

Buffinton

6

SWANSEA

6

Gardners Neck

138

Long

Barton

103

Seaview

MOUNT HOPE BAY

Touisset Point

Elm

North

DIGHTON

138

Water

Pleasant

Avon

SOMERSET

South

Main

Riverside

Taunton River

HOW to get there

From I–195, take exit 3 (Route 6) and go east for 0.5 mile to McDonald's on left, in shopping center.

- Right out of *back* of shopping center onto Milford Road. *Caution:* Speed bumps. Go 0.6 mile to end (Hortonville Road).
- Right and just ahead left at traffic light on Main Street. Notice dam on left as you turn left. Go 2.8 miles to traffic light at bottom of hill (County Street, Route 138).

- Straight for 0.3 mile to end (Riverside Avenue) at Taunton River.
- Turn left and stay on main road for 1.5 miles to South Street, which bears right uphill.
- Bear right for 0.4 mile to end (Main Street, unmarked).
- Left for 0.5 mile to Avon Street on left.
- Left and just ahead right at grassy traffic island on Pleasant Street (unmarked). Go 0.7 mile to crossroads (North Street). Here the 13-mile ride turns left.
- Straight for 1.8 miles to Water Street, a little lane on right just after small bridge with concrete abutments.
- Right for 0.6 mile to blinking light (Route 138, County Street).
- Go straight for 0.4 mile to crossroads (Elm Street). Notice graceful church a little to your right at crossroads.
- Left for 3 miles to end (Whetstone Hill Road on left, Marvel Street on right). Tough hill at the beginning.
- Right for 1 mile to crossroads and blinking light (Sharps Lot Road). Here the 17-mile ride goes straight.
- Right for 1.7 miles to crossroads (Williams Street on right, Baker Road on left).
- Left for 1.6 miles to end (Hornbine Road). There's a one-room schoolhouse at the intersection.
- Left for 0.5 mile to Spring Street on right.
- Right for 1 mile to fork where the main road bears left and Martin Street (unmarked) turns right.
- Bear left on main road for 0.2 mile to end (Route 118).
- Left for 0.8 mile to end (Locust Street). Water tower on right at end.
- Right for 1.8 miles to end (Old Fall River Road).

- Left for 0.8 mile to stop sign (merge left on Route 6).
- Bear left and then immediately turn right on Bushee Road, unmarked (*Caution* here). Go 1.4 miles to end (Schoolhouse Road).
- Left for 0.2 mile to Long Lane on right.
- Right for 0.2 mile to crossroads and stop sign (Route 103).
- Straight for 2.6 miles to traffic light (Route 103 again, Wilbur Avenue), staying on main road. (After 1.8 mile you can turn right at the bay onto Seaview Avenue; it runs along the water for 1 mile to dead end.)
- Right for 1.3 miles to blinking light at top of hill (Gardners Neck Road, unmarked).
- Left (*Caution* here) for 0.9 mile to traffic light (Route 6, G.A.R. Highway).
- Straight for 0.6 mile to Milford Road on left, shortly after traffic light.
- Left for 0.6 mile to back entrance to shopping center on left. *Caution:* Speed bumps just after you turn into entrance.

17 miles

- Follow first 12 directions of long ride, to Sharps Lot Road.
- Straight for 1.8 miles to end (merge left at stop sign).
- Bear left for 0.5 mile to Milford Road on right.
- Right for 0.6 mile to back entrance of shopping center on left. *Caution:* Speed bumps just after you turn into entrance.

13 miles

- Follow first 7 directions of long ride, to North Street.
- Left for 0.3 mile to crossroads and stop sign (Route 138).
- Straight for 0.7 mile to end (Elm Street, unmarked). You'll pass the Somerset Reservoir hidden behind an embankment on your left.
- Left for 1 mile to end (Whetstone Hill Road on left).
- Right for 1 mile to crossroads and blinking light (Sharps Lot Road).
- Follow last 3 directions of 16-mile ride.

From Dighton the short ride heads back toward Swansea along a ridge with impressive views of the river and the surrounding landscape. The longer ride heads farther inland to Rehoboth, a beautiful rural town of farms and winding, wooded roads. You'll pass the Hornbine School, a one-room schoolhouse built during the 1830s and used until 1934. Cross briefly into a little strip of Rhode Island to the shore of Mount Hope Bay, just back over the Massachusetts line. After a scenic, curving ride along the shore, it's a short distance back to the start.

Barrington Ride

Number of miles: 15

Terrain: Flat.

Start: Commuter parking lot, Routes 114 and 103 (County Road), Barrington.

Food: Convenience store at corner of Washington Road and Bay Spring Avenue. Newport Creamery and Friendly's on County Road.

Facilities: Portable toilet on bike path just west of Narragansett Avenue.

CAUTION:

The East Bay Bicycle Path is very heavily used in good weather by both cyclists and noncyclists. Please read *Caution* in the "Bikeways" section of the introduction.

On this ride, one of the flattest and most relaxing in the book, you'll explore Barrington, a well-to-do suburb of Providence on the eastern shore of Narragansett Bay. The route abounds with tranquil rides along the water and goes past Barrington Beach, a good spot for a swim on a hot day. Two parts of the ride follow sections of the lovely East Bay Bicycle Path.

The ride starts next to the stately white church overlooking the Barrington River. Cross the bridge and enjoy a lovely ride along the river. Cross the river again and continue to follow it on Mathewson Road, an idyllic lane from which you can see the church spires and picturesque old wharves of the town of Warren, on the opposite bank.

Turn westward toward Narragansett Bay. Barrington Beach, tucked away at the end of a side street, is a pleasant spot for a rest. Just ahead, pedal through the Rhode Island Country Club, with lush green fairways sloping gently from the road to the bay. As you approach Nayatt Point, gracious homes with beautifully landscaped grounds keep watch along the shore.

The route turns inland briefly to go alongside unspoiled Echo Lake and then dips down to the bay once again. Go around Allens Neck, where you have fine views of the water. Just ahead is Haines Memorial State Park, a pleasant picnic spot that extends down to Bullocks Cove, an inlet of the bay. Near the end of the ride, pedal for about 3 miles along the East Bay Bicycle Path, which hugs the shore of Brickyard Pond. In the center of town, you will see the elegant stone town hall, built in 1888, on Route 103.

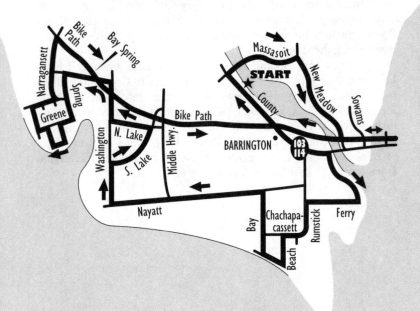

HOW **to get there**
From the north, exit south from I–195 onto Route 114 (exit 7). Go about 5.5 miles to traffic light with big white church on far left corner. Parking lot is on left just after church.

From the east, exit west from I–195 onto Route 103 (exit 4A), toward Warren. Go about 6 miles to Route 114 in downtown Warren. Right for about 2.5 miles to parking lot on right, just before church.

By bike from Providence, head east on Waterman Street. Right on Gano Street. Right on bicycle ramp that leads up to I–195 overpass. Cross Seekonk River bridge on sidewalk. At far end of bridge, cross Warren Avenue onto First Street. Go 2 blocks to East Bay Bicycle Path on right. Follow bike path about 7.5 miles to County Road (Routes 114 and 103) at traffic light. There's a shopping center on right at the intersection. Left for 1 mile to parking lot on right.

- Right out of parking lot to traffic light just ahead.
- Right for 0.8 mile to end (New Meadow Road).
- Right for 1.2 miles to East Bay Bicycle Path, just before end.
- Left for 0.5 mile to small crossroads with rocks at each corner, shortly after wooden bridge. *Caution:* Bike path is very heavily used in good weather. Please read *Caution* in the "Bike-ways" section of the introduction.
- Make U-turn and follow bike path 1 mile to traffic light (County Road). The light is activated by a push button.
- Left for 0.4 mile to Mathewson Road, immediately before bridge.
- Right for 1.5 miles to end (Rumstick Road, unmarked).
- Left for 0.3 mile to stop sign where main road curves sharply right and small road goes straight.
- Curve right. Just ahead the main road curves sharply left, but go straight on Chachapacassett Road (unmarked) for 0.3 mile to Beach Road on left, at bottom of hill.
- Left for 0.1 mile to water. Walk bike around barricade and turn right along water (Barrington Beach) for 1 block to stop sign.
- Bear right uphill on Bay Street (unmarked) for 0.4 mile to end (Nayatt Road).
- Left for 1.3 miles to where the main road turns right on Washington Road and a smaller road goes straight.
- Right for 0.3 mile to South Lake Drive (unmarked), a narrow lane on right at bottom of hill.
- Right for 0.5 mile to crossroads and stop sign (North Lake Drive, unmarked). *Caution:* Bumpy spots.
- Left for 0.4 mile to end (Washington Road, unmarked).
- Right for 0.6 mile to Bay Spring Avenue on left.
- Left for 0.4 mile to Spring Avenue on left, opposite lace mill. You'll pass an old brick mill on your left that has been renovated into apartments.
- Left for 0.3 mile to end (Greene Avenue, unmarked).
- Right for 1 short block to crossroads and stop sign.

- Left for 0.2 mile to crossroads and stop sign (Greene Avenue again).
- Left and just ahead right at end (Shore Drive, unmarked). Go 1 block to end (Latham Avenue, unmarked).
- Right and just ahead left at crossroads and stop sign (Narragansett Avenue). Go 0.4 mile to East Bay Bicycle Path. Haines Memorial State Park on both sides of road at intersection.
- Right on bike path for 2.8 miles to County Road (Route 103), at traffic light, which is activated by a push button. *Caution* again on the bike path.
- Left for 1 mile to parking lot on right. Historic town hall on right after 0.2 mile.

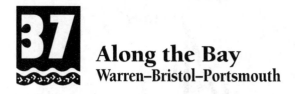

Along the Bay
Warren–Bristol–Portsmouth

Number of miles:	10 (18 with downtown Bristol extension, 24 with Portsmouth loop)
Terrain:	Flat, with two short hills and a long, steady climb on Bayview Avenue. The long ride has a tough climb up to and then over the Mount Hope Bridge.
Start:	Commuter parking lot, Franklin Street, Warren. It's just south of the center of town and just east of Route 114.
Food:	Several grocery stores and snack bars en route. Flo's Clam Shack, opposite the waterfront in Portsmouth, is a classic snack bar that has been around since the 1930s.
Facilities:	Portable toilet at junction of East Bay Bicycle Path and Asylum Road, in Colt State Park.

CAUTION:
The East Bay Bicycle Path is very heavily used in good weather by both cyclists and noncyclists. Please read *Caution* in the "Bikeways" section of the introduction.

Fine views of Narragansett and Mount Hope Bays abound on this flat, scenic ride. The historic town of Bristol commands a peninsula poised between Narragansett Bay on the west and Mount Hope Bay on the east. Highlights of the ride include a lovely section of the East Bay Bicycle Path between Warren and Bristol and a spin through Colt State Park, a magnificent, well-maintained former estate with an ex-

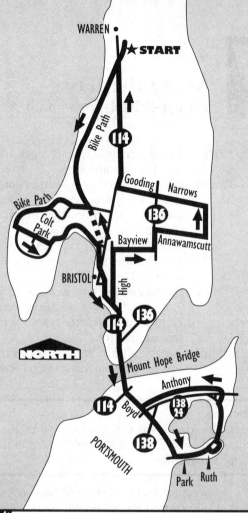

WARREN

★ START

Bike Path

114

Gooding — Narrows

Bike Path

Colt Park

136

Bayview — Annawamscutt

BRISTOL

High

114   136

NORTH

Mount Hope Bridge

Anthony

114   Boyd

138
24

PORTSMOUTH

138

Park   Ruth

HOW to get there Exit south from I–195 onto Route 136. Just ahead, cross Route 6 at traffic light. Continue 3.2 miles to Franklin Street on right, at traffic light (it's immediately after a one-way section). Right for 0.5 mile to parking lot on right.

By bike from Providence, get onto East Bay Bicycle Path (see Ride 36). Follow bike path about 9.5 miles to parking lot next to path on left.

DIREC-TIONS
for the ride

10 & 24 miles

- Left (south) on bike path, which runs next to parking lot. Just ahead cross Route 114 at traffic light that is activated by a push button. Continue on bike path for 2.7 miles to divided parkway (Asylum Road, unmarked). You will now go through Colt State Park. *Caution:* Bike path is very heavily used in good weather. Please read *Caution* in the "Bikeways" section of the introduction.

- Right for 100 yards to where main road bears left and side road goes straight.

- Straight for 0.8 mile to bridge over inlet. (*Caution* at speed bumps and at barricades to keep out cars.)

- Bear right immediately after bridge. Just ahead bear right again for 50 feet to bike path directly next to bay.

- Bear left, following bay on right. Go 0.8 mile to automobile road, just after you curve left away from water.

- Cross automobile road and go 0.2 mile to where bike path turns 90 degrees left and grassy path goes straight, at top of hill.

- Walk bike along grassy path (stone mansion on left). After 100 yards, continue straight on paved road for 0.4 mile to end (Poppasquash Road, unmarked). Road may be barricaded to cars at beginning.

- Left for 1.2 miles to bike path, which crosses road just before end. (For 10-mile ride, turn left on bike path and follow it 3.4 miles to parking lot on right, just after you cross Route 114.)

- Right for 0.3 mile to end of bike path, just before Independence Park. (The route now goes through downtown Bristol on Route 114. If you prefer to avoid downtown traffic, continue straight on road along bay for 0.6 mile, turn left immediately before dead end for 1 block to Route 114, and right for 1.7 miles to beginning of Mount Hope Bridge.)

- Turn 90 degrees left on Oliver Street and just ahead right at stop sign on Route 114. Go 2.3 miles to beginning of Mount Hope Bridge. Here the 18-mile ride makes a U-turn. (*Caution:* Watch for car doors opening into your path in downtown area. If you want to look at the buildings, it's safest to walk your bike a few blocks.)

- Cross bridge to traffic light at far end. (*Caution:* It's safest to walk your bike across the expansion joints.)
- Bear left for 0.7 mile to traffic light (Route 138).
- Straight for 0.4 mile to end. (*Caution:* Most of the traffic coming up behind you will bear right on Route 138.)
- Left for 0.7 mile to Ruth Avenue on right, opposite Island Tap.
- Right for 0.2 mile to third left (Ivy Avenue, unmarked); it's a dead end if you go straight. Left for 100 feet to end.
- Right for 0.9 mile to unmarked road on right at a large, grassy traffic island (sign says TO COMMON FENCE POINT).
- Right for 1.5 miles to end, after motel on left.
- Right for 0.4 mile to traffic light, and bear right across bridge.
- At far end of bridge continue 0.3 mile to fork (Route 136 bears right, Route 114 bears left).
- Bear left and stay on Route 114 for 0.9 mile to High Street on right, immediately before blinking light.
- Right for 1 mile to Bayview Avenue on right, just before end.
- Right for 0.8 mile to traffic light at top of hill (Route 136, Metacom Avenue). This is a steady climb.
- Left for 0.5 mile to Annawamscutt Drive on right, about 100 yards before traffic light. *Caution:* Route 136 is very busy.
- Right for 0.9 mile to King Philip Avenue (unmarked) on left, immediately before dead end at bay.
- Left for 0.5 mile to end (Narrows Road, unmarked).
- Left for 0.9 mile to traffic light (Route 136, Metacom Avenue).
- Straight for 0.8 mile to end (Route 114).
- Right for 2.2 miles to bike path, at traffic light. Bear right for 100 yards to parking lot on right.

18 miles

- Follow long ride to beginning of Mount Hope Bridge.

- Make a U-turn and go 0.3 mile to fork (Route 136 bears right, Route 114 bears left).
- Follow last 9 directions of long ride.

---

tensive waterfront on Narragansett Bay. The park was originally owned by Samuel P. Colt, nephew of the inventor of the Colt revolver.

The beginning of the ride follows one of the most scenic sections of the East Bay Bicycle Path, which skirts the bay fairly closely between Warren and Colt State Park. The bike path, which was formerly a Providence & Worcester railroad line, is completely flat. Leave the bike path and enter Colt State Park, where you'll pedal directly along the shoreline for over a mile. Pass the handsome stone main mansion (built as a barn), guarded by two bronze lions. Just ahead is the Coggeshall Farm Museum, a working restoration of an eighteenth-century farm. The 10-mile ride follows the bike path back to Warren.

Beyond the park, the road winds along Bristol Harbor. A mile later go through the center of town, passing handsome nineteenth-century schools, churches, and mansions. One of the mansions, Linden Place (at 500 Hope Street), is open limited hours. It was built in 1810.

South of downtown, follow the harbor to the tip of the peninsula. You pass Blithewold, a Newport-style mansion with extensive landscaped grounds and gardens. It was formerly the summer residence of Augustus VanWickle, a Pennsylvania coal magnate. At the tip of the peninsula, the bold, modern campus of Roger Williams University stands guard above Mount Hope Bay.

The 18-mile ride returns along High Street, which is graced by several elegant homes originally owned by sea captains and an impressive cluster of nineteenth-century schools and churches. To finish the ride, climb to the spine of the peninsula and descend to Mount Hope Bay. Hug the shoreline on a quiet residential street, then turn west to Route 114, which leads back to the starting point.

The 24-mile ride leaves Bristol to cross the spectacular, mile-long Mount Hope Bridge to Portsmouth. On a clear day, the view from the top is unparalleled, and you should dismount to fully savor it. In Portsmouth, ride along the head of the broad Sakonnet River, passing the remains of the stone bridge that used to span the narrowest point between Portsmouth and Tiverton. The center span of the bridge collapsed during the 1938 hurricane and was replaced by the Sakonnet Bridge, a mile to the north. The waterfront community here, called Island Park, maintains a 1950s ambience with its closely clustered former beach cottages and neighborhood snack bars and taverns. Head back to the Mount Hope Bridge to rejoin the 18-mile ride.

From Bristol Harbor you can take the ferry to Prudence Island in the middle of Narragansett Bay. This is a peaceful spot with some summer homes and large expanses of undeveloped woodland, roamed by deer, at the north and south ends. For information on ferry schedules call Prudence Island Ferry, (401) 253–9808.

Jamestown Ride

Number of miles:	17 (26 with Fort Getty–Beavertail extension)
Terrain:	Rolling, with several short steep hills. The long ride has an additional hill at the beginning of Beavertail Road.
Road Surface:	Less than 0.2 mile of dirt road, which can be avoided.
Start:	Jamestown Community Playground, corner of North Main Road and Valley Street, in Jamestown.
Food:	Restaurant in the center of town. Grocery on Southwest Avenue, 2 blocks south of start.

The island of Jamestown, which guards the mouth of Narragansett Bay between Newport and the mainland, is a most enjoyable spot for bicycling. As you pedal around the slender island, less than 2 miles across at its widest point, views of the bay emerge around every bend. Because Jamestown's population is small and a cross-island expressway has been constructed, traffic on the side roads is very light.

The ride starts from the southern part of the island about a half mile from the center of town. At the beginning you'll come to the intersection with Narragansett Avenue, which heads toward the center of town. Here the ride goes straight ahead, but if you turn left you can visit the Jamestown Museum, a nineteenth-century schoolhouse with memorabilia from the old ferries (pre-dating the bridges) and other items of local interest. It's the first building on the left after you turn left.

The short ride now continues on Highland Drive, along the southern shore of the main part of the island. This narrow, curving lane bobs up and down little hills, passing rambling cedar-shingled

homes with gables and turrets overlooking the rocky ledges along the shore. Just ahead is Fort Wetherill State Park, a magnificent spot worth exploring. The fort, built between 1899 and 1906, is a massive structure on a cliff overlooking the bay, complete with turrets, ramparts, underground ammunition rooms, and mysterious narrow tunnels. The complex housed hundreds of troops during the two World Wars. Next to the fort are little roads looping around the adjoining cliffs.

Head north along the eastern side of the island, passing Jamestown Harbor and pedaling underneath the Newport Bridge. As you bike along the northern half of the island, which is less developed than the southern half, the road ascends onto low ridges, with fields and gentleman farms sloping to the bay a couple of hundred yards away. As you curve south for the return leg, you go inland through a wooded area, descend sharply to the western shore, and then ride directly along the shoreline with the graceful arch of the Jamestown–Verrazano Bridge always in view.

After passing underneath the bridge, you'll ascend a gradual rise. On your right is the Watson Farm, a working farm complete with barnyard animals, that is open to visitors. At the top there is an old windmill on the left, dating from 1787. Restored to operating condition by the Jamestown Historical Society, it is open to visitors on weekend afternoons during the summer. You'll cross a salt marsh just before the end of the ride.

The long ride includes the narrow peninsula that extends to the southwest below the main part of the island. First head toward Fort Getty, a small headland on the west shore with some old fortifications and a campground. Then proceed south to Beavertail Point at the tip of the peninsula. The point, a state park, is a spectacular rocky promontory with a granite lighthouse built in 1856. Adjoining the lighthouse is a small museum that traces its history. On windy days, the surf crashes onto the rocks with an awe-inspiring display of natural forces. Return to the main part of the island, passing through open fields and moors. Just past the causeway along Mackerel Cove, between the Beavertail peninsula and the main portion of the island, you rejoin the long ride on Highland Drive.

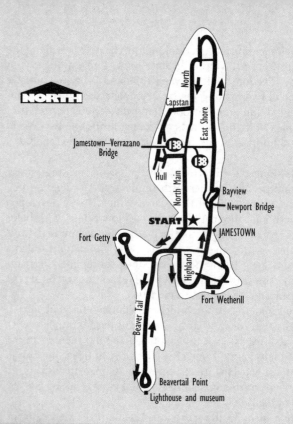

NORTH

North
Capstan
East Shore
Jamestown–Verrazano
Bridge
138
138
Hull
North Main
Bayview
Newport Bridge
START
JAMESTOWN
Fort Getty
Highland
Beaver Tail
Fort Wetherill
Beavertail Point
Lighthouse and museum

HOW to get there From the north, head south on I–95 and Routes 4 and 1 to Route 138 East. Go east on Route 138 for 3 miles to bridge. Take the first exit after the birdge (Helm Street). At stop sign, go straight for 0.6 mile to end. Right for 1.9 miles to playground on left. Park in lot on far side of playground.

From the south, exit east from I-95 onto Route 138 and follow it to bridge. Proceed as above.

From the east, cross the Newport Bridge (Route 138) from Newport to Jamestown. Bear right immediately after toll booth (sign says TO JAMESTOWN) for 0.4 mile to end. Left for 0.8 mile to stop sign in center of town. Right for 0.4 mile to stop sign and blinking light (North Main Road). Right for 0.1 mile to playground on right. Park on far side of playground.

DIREC-TIONS
for the ride

26 miles

- Left on North Main Road for 0.1 mile to stop sign and blinking light (Narragansett Avenue).
- Straight for 0.6 mile to where you merge with a road coming in on the left at a sharp angle (Hamilton Avenue). Here the short ride turns sharply left.
- Bear right for 0.4 mile to first right (sign says FORT GETTY). *Caution:* Bumpy road.
- Right for 1 mile to tip of peninsula. Person in gatehouse will usually allow bikes through for free. Make a small counterclockwise loop around camping area and return along the same road to end (Beavertail Road, unmarked).
- Right for 2.8 miles to fork, just before lighthouse at tip of Beavertail Point. (When you leave the park, you will return along Beavertail Road, the same road that leads to it.)
- Bear right at fork, go past lighthouse, and continue for 0.6 mile to another fork (sign points right to exit).
- Bear right out of park for 2.7 miles to fork just past causeway.
- Bear slightly right for 100 yards to Highland Drive on right.
- Right for 1.4 miles to grassy traffic island immediately before stop sign.
- Turn right and immediately bear right at stop sign. Go 0.2 mile to entrance to Fort Wetherill State Park, on right.
- Right into park and explore it on one-way loops. The fort is at far end of the loop farthest up the hill. Leave park at entrance 0.2 mile east of first one, at bottom of hill.
- Left out of park and immediately right on Dumpling Drive. Go 0.3 mile to fork. *Caution:* This stretch is very bumpy and gravelly. It is safest to walk your bike.
- Bear right for 0.5 mile to end, at top of hill. This section is dirt for 0.2 mile. To avoid it, bear left instead of right for 0.3 mile to end, at top of hill.
- Right for 1.1 mile to fork where main road bears left and Bayview Drive (unmarked) bears right along bay. You'll go through the center of Jamestown.

221

- Bear right for 0.7 mile to second stop sign, and bear right downhill for 0.1 mile to end (East Shore Road, unmarked).
- Turn right at end, following the bay closely on your right. Continue straight along the bay for 4.6 miles to stop sign (Summit Avenue). The main road bears left here. (Don't get on the new Route 138 West, a divided highway.)
- Bear left for 0.4 mile to crossroads and stop sign (North Road, unmarked). A dirt road goes straight here. *Caution:* This section is bumpy.
- Right for 1.3 miles to Capstan Street on right, midway up hill.
- Right for 1.5 miles to fork (Beach Avenue bears left). *Caution:* After 0.5 mile there's a steep descent with a sandy, 90-degree left turn at the bottom. Please take it easy.
- Straight along the bay for 0.6 mile to first left after going underneath bridges (Hull Street).
- Left for 0.3 mile to end (Helm Street, unmarked).
- Left and just ahead right at end for 0.6 mile to end (North Road on left, North Main Road on right).
- Right for 1.9 miles to playground on left.

17 miles

- Follow first 2 directions of long ride.
- Sharp left on Hamilton Avenue for 100 yards to Highland Drive on right.
- Follow last 15 directions of long ride, beginning "Right for 1.4 miles to grassy traffic island . . ."

Middletown–Portsmouth
Aquidneck Island Central

Number of miles:	15
Terrain:	Gently rolling, with one hill on Third Beach Road.
Start:	Portsmouth Middle School, Jepson Lane in Portsmouth, Rhode Island.
Food:	None on route.
Caution:	This ride has two half-mile sections on Route 138, a busy, undivided four-lane highway with no shoulders. Ride in the middle of the right lane rather than at the edge so that traffic must pass you in the left lane. It's safest to ride early in the morning, before the traffic builds up.

Aquidneck Island, which is officially the island of Rhode Island, contains the communities of Portsmouth in the north, Middletown in the middle, and Newport in the south. Long and slender, the island is 15 miles long from tip to tip and 5 miles across at its widest point. Magnificently situated in the center of Narragansett Bay, with broad stretches of open farmland sloping gently down to the shore, Aquidneck Island contains some of the finest biking territory in the state.

This ride starts from about halfway down the island, just north of the Portsmouth–Middletown line. Begin by pedaling south along Jepson Lane, where broad expanses of open land stretch for acres on both sides of the road. On your left you can see Sisson Pond, a couple hundred yards off the road. Occasional new homes, stark-looking against the treeless landscape, dot the roadside. As the population of the island grows, due primarily to expanding high-tech industries

conducting research for the Navy, more and more new houses are going up on what was once unspoiled farmland. Fortunately, most of the island is still undeveloped.

As you head south on Berkeley Avenue and Paradise Road, the landscape becomes more gracious in appearance, with gentleman farms bordered by orderly, squared-off stone walls and gateposts. You'll pass Whitehall, the 1729 mansion of philosopher and educator George Berkeley. About a mile ahead you'll pass the Paradise School, a charming Victorian schoolhouse complete with a bell tower, built in 1875. Dominating the horizon ahead of you is the Gothic spire of the Saint George's School Chapel, which is worth visiting. If you'd like to see it, bear right instead of left at the end of Paradise Road, curve right while going up the hill, and turn right into the school at the top.

Paradise Road leads all the way down to the ocean at Second Beach, which is refreshingly undeveloped and uncommercialized. Bike along the beach and cross the narrow neck to Third Beach. Between the two beaches, at the southeast corner of the island, lies Sachuest Point, an unspoiled sandy peninsula that is a National Wildlife Reserve. If you'd like to visit it, bear right instead of left at the end of Second Beach, adding about 2.5 miles to the ride.

Head north along Third Beach and just ahead pass the Norman Audubon Sanctuary, a lovely expanse of fields and woodland. At the northern end of the route you'll ride past Glen Farm, a major center for equestrian sports in Rhode Island. To finish the ride, head west across the island on Union Street, which runs alongside Saint Mary's Pond.

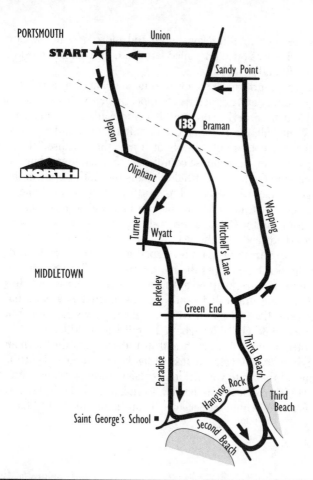

PORTSMOUTH

Union

START ★

Sandy Point

Jepson

138 Braman

NORTH

Oliphant

Wapping

Turner

Wyatt

Mitchell's Lane

MIDDLETOWN

Berkeley

Green End

Paradise

Third Beach

Hanging Rock

Third
Beach

Saint George's School ■

Second Beach

HOW From the north, take Route 114 south to Union Street on left,
to get at traffic light. It's 3 miles south of the end of Route 24 or 6 miles
there south of the Mount Hope Bridge. Turn left on Union Street and
take first right on Jepson Lane. The school is just ahead on the right.

   From the south, cross the Newport Bridge and exit north on Route 138.
Go 0.5 mile to Route 114 and the traffic light. Turn left on Route 114 and go
about 4 miles to Union Street on the right, at traffic light. Turn right on
Union Street and take your first right on Jepson Lane. The school is just
ahead on the right.

- Right on Jepson Lane for 1.3 miles to end (Oliphant Lane).
- Left for 0.5 mile to end (Route 138).
- Right for 0.5 mile to Turner Road (unmarked), which bears left at gas station.
- Bear left (use *extreme caution* here) for 0.3 mile to crossroads and stop sign (Wyatt Road, unmarked).
- Left for 0.2 mile to Berkeley Avenue on right.
- Right for 0.9 mile to another crossroads and stop sign (Green End Avenue, unmarked).
- Continue straight for 1.3 miles to fork at bottom of hill.
- Bear left and just ahead bear left again at end. Go 0.3 mile to fork.
- Bear right for 0.4 mile to another fork, where a smaller road bears left (sign may point left to Third Beach).
- Bear left for 0.2 mile to another fork.
- Bear left and just ahead bear left again at yield sign. Go 0.4 mile to crossroads and stop sign (Hanging Rock Road on left, Indian Avenue on right). *Caution:* Bumpy and sandy spots.
- Straight for 1 mile to crossroads and stop sign (Green End Avenue, unmarked).
- Continue straight for 0.3 mile to yield sign where Mitchell's Lane bears left and Wapping Road turns right.
- Right for 2.9 miles to end (Sandy Point Road).
- Left for 0.5 mile to end (Route 138).
- Right for 0.5 mile to Union Street (unmarked) on left, immediately after state police station on left.
- Left (use *extreme caution* here) for 1.6 miles to Jepson Lane on left, shortly before traffic light.
- Left for 0.2 mile to school on right.

Newport–Middletown
Aquidneck Island South

Number of miles:	18 (26 with Middletown extension)
Terrain:	Flat, with one hill on the longer ride.
Start:	Burger King on Route 114 in Middletown, just north of Route 138 East.
Food:	Numerous snack bars in Newport. Burger King at end.
Caution:	On summer weekends, traffic along the harbor, Ocean Drive, and the mansion area is very heavy. The best time to bike during the summer is early morning.

Newport is the scenic, historic, and architectural pinnacle of Rhode Island. The city contains mansions of incredible opulence once owned by Vanderbilts and Astors and narrow streets lined with historic homes and public buildings. The bustling waterfront is complete with boutiques, haute-cuisine restaurants, and docks with sleek yachts moored beside them. For several miles, magnificent Ocean Drive runs along the rocky shoreline passing mansion after mansion. Many mansions offer guided tours to the public, and most are located on Bellevue Avenue. The largest and most ornate mansion of all is The Breakers on Ochre Point Avenue, formerly owned by the Vanderbilts. Rosecliff, not far behind in opulence, was the setting for part of the movie *The Great Gatsby*.

The ride starts by skirting the Newport Naval Base, one of the largest in the country until it was largely deactivated during the 1970s. The Naval War College Museum, which features exhibits on the history of naval warfare and the naval heritage of Narragansett Bay, is located here. You pass under the Newport Bridge, one of the longest and most impressive on the East Coast; unfortunately bikes are not allowed on the bridge itself, because of wheel-eating expansion joints. Go along the harbor, lined with hundreds of boats and yachts, and pass Fort Adams State Park, with its massive fortification overlooking Newport Harbor. The Museum of Yachting is located in the park. Just past Fort Adams is Hammersmith Farm, an estate formerly owned by the Auchincloss family, the parents of Jacqueline Kennedy Onassis, and now open to the public. John F. Kennedy and Jacqueline had their wedding reception here, and later the estate was used as a summer White House.

A little farther along Ocean Drive is Brenton Point State Park, containing a magnificent stretch of coastline. It is a favorite spot for flying kites. You pass by Rosecliff, The Breakers, and Salve Regina University. The campus, perched on ocean-front cliffs and surrounded by mansions, is one of the most spectacularly situated in the country. Passing behind the mansions is the Cliff Walk, a footpath along the coast running from Memorial Boulevard to the promontory south of Bellevue Avenue. You can walk your bike along the northern half, but the path becomes progressively rougher south of Rosecliff.

Just beyond the mansion area you'll descend to gently curving Easton Beach (often called First Beach), a good spot for a swim. The road along the beach is a causeway, with the ocean on the right and Easton Pond on the left. Just ahead the short ride turns north, hugging the shore of the pond to return to the starting point.

The long ride heads farther east into Middletown, which provides a tranquil contrast to the bustle and opulence of Newport. You continue to follow the shore to Purgatory Chasm, a narrow cleft in the cliffs overlooking the ocean, and then Second Beach. You bike past Saint Columba's Church, a graceful stone structure with a small cemetery beside it. After following the ocean for another mile, head inland back to the starting point, pedaling through broad expanses of open farmland.

In an area as historically and architecturally significant as Newport, it is impossible to put all points of interest on the route without turning it into a labyrinth. I have elected to follow the water, one of

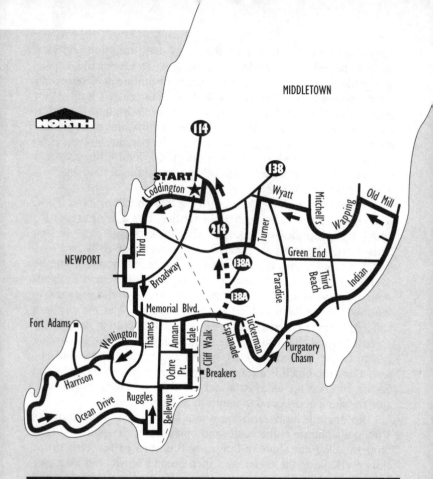

NORTH

MIDDLETOWN

START

NEWPORT

Fort Adams

HOW to get there From the Providence area, head east on I–195 and exit south on Route 24 to end (Route 114). Straight for about 6 miles to Burger King on left, immediately before traffic light.

From the Fall River or Taunton area and north, head south on Route 24 to end (Route 114). Proceed as above.

From the east, head west on I–195 and exit south on Route 24 to end (Route 114). Proceed as above.

From the west, head east on Route 138 to fork where Route 138 bears right and Route 114 goes straight. Straight for 0.1 mile to Burger King on right.

DIRECTIONS for the ride

26 miles

- Right out of *side* entrance to Burger King, and immediately cross Route 114 at traffic light onto Coddington Highway. Go 0.8 mile to fork (main road bears left).
- Bear left for 0.7 mile to rotary.
- Right for 0.1 mile to first left, at traffic light (Third Street, unmarked). Here the ride turns left, but if you'd like to visit the Naval War College Museum go straight for 0.4 mile to museum on right. There may be a guard at the entrance to the Naval War College; he will let you through if you say you are visiting the museum. Stay on the road to the museum—the rest of the Naval War College is not open to the public.
- Turn left at traffic light (right if you visited the museum). Go 0.5 mile to Sycamore Street on right, immediately after you go under Newport Bridge.
- Right for 0.9 mile to end (America's Cup Avenue, an unmarked divided road), passing bridge to Goat Island and Doubletree Hotel.
- Right for 0.4 mile to Thames Street, at traffic light (post office on far left corner). Docks are worth exploring. Immediately before the intersection, on the right, notice the sculpture of a swimmer diving into a wave, with only the feet protruding.
- Right along harbor for 0.5 mile to Wellington Avenue (unmarked), at traffic island. It's opposite a gas station on left.
- Right for 0.8 mile to crossroads and stop sign (Harrison Avenue).
- Right for 0.4 mile to end, opposite Independence Square (a center for the rehabilitation of persons with disabilities).
- Right for 0.5 mile to entrance road to Fort Adams (worth visiting). The Museum of Yachting is located here.
- Straight for 0.4 mile to fork (Ridge Road bears right).
- Bear right for 4.6 miles to end, at traffic island. Ridge Road becomes Ocean Drive.
- Turn right. Just ahead road turns 90 degrees left on Bellevue Avenue (unmarked). Go 1.1 miles to small crossroads just past Rosecliff (Ruggles Avenue). A sign may point right to The Breakers.

- Right for 0.4 mile to second left, Ochre Point Avenue. If you wish, continue to end (nice view), left on the Cliff Walk, and *walk* your bike 1.2 miles to end (Memorial Boulevard). Resume ride there (4 directions ahead).
- Left on Ochre Point Avenue for 0.5 mile to end, passing The Breakers and the campus of Salve Regina University.
- Left for 0.1 mile to first right (Annandale Road).
- Right for 0.6 mile to end (Memorial Boulevard).
- Right for 1.1 miles to Route 138A, which bears left. Here short ride bears left.
- Straight for 0.1 mile to Tuckerman Avenue, which bears right.
- Bear right and immediately right again on Esplanade. Go 0.2 mile to first left at stop sign.
- Left and just ahead right at stop sign (Tuckerman Avenue again). Go 1 mile to stop sign (merge right on Purgatory Avenue, unmarked). Purgatory Chasm (unmarked) on right just before stop sign.
- Bear right and just ahead bear right again at bottom of hill. Go 0.4 mile to fork (Hanging Rock Road, unmarked, bears left).
- Bear left for 0.8 mile to crossroads and stop sign (Third Beach Road, umarked).
- Straight for 1.9 miles to Old Mill Lane, at DEAD END sign.
- Left for 0.7 mile to end (Wapping Road, unmarked).
- Turn left and stay on main road for 1.5 miles to Wyatt Road on left, at stop sign.
- Left for 0.8 mile to crossroads and stop sign (Turner Road).
- Left for 0.9 mile to end (Green End Avenue, unmarked).
- Right for 0.6 mile to second traffic light (Route 214, Valley Road), at bottom of hill.
- Right for 0.9 mile to traffic light (Route 138).
- Straight for less than 0.4 mile to parking lot for Knights of Columbus hall on left, just before end.
- Turn left into parking lot (*Caution* here). Go to far right corner of lot, and walk bike around a barricade onto a street that is perpendicular to the road you were just on.

- Follow this street (Ridgewood Road, unmarked) for 0.4 mile to Burger King on right, immediately before traffic light. *Caution:* The first block is bumpy.

18 miles

- Follow first 18 directions of long ride, to junction of Memorial Boulevard and Route 138A.
- Bear left on Route 138A for 0.4 mile to traffic light, where Route 214 (unmarked) bears left.
- Bear left for 2.1 miles to parking lot for Knights of Columbus hall on left, just before end. You'll go straight at 2 traffic lights.
- Follow last 2 directions of long ride.

---

the city's most visually appealing features. The center of town and many historic landmarks are 2 or 3 blocks inland and are best seen on foot.

Tiverton–Little Compton

Number of miles:	17 (25 with Little Compton extension, 35 with Westport–Adamsville extension)
Terrain:	Gently rolling, with two steady, gradual climbs, and one long hill on the 35-mile ride.
Start:	Commuter parking lot on Fish Road, Tiverton, immediately north of Route 24. Turn right at end of exit ramp if you're heading south on Route 24.
Food:	Country store and small restaurant in Little Compton. Gray's Ice Cream, corner of Routes 179 and 77, Tiverton (17-mile ride). Country store and Abraham Manchester's Restaurant in Adamsville.

The southeastern corner of the state, spanning the slender strip of land between the eastern shore of Narragansett Bay and the Massachusetts state line, is the best area of its size in Rhode Island for cycling. The region is a pedaler's paradise of untraveled country lanes winding past salt marshes, snug, cedar-shingled homes with immaculately tended lawns, trim picket fences, and broad meadows sloping down to the bay. The center of Little Compton is the finest traditional New England village in the state.

Tiverton, a gracious town hugging the shore of the mile-wide Sakonnet River, is an attractive place to start the ride. Descend steeply to the river, follow it closely on Route 77, and then turn onto idyllic, narrow country lanes that hug the river. Seapowet Avenue crosses a small inlet over a rustic, wooden-railed bridge. Two miles ahead go along lovely Nonquit Pond. The short ride now returns to Tiverton inland from the river on wooded back roads. Gray's Ice Cream is an excellent halfway stop.

The 25-mile ride follows Route 77 south, climbing onto a ridge with dramatic views of broad meadows sloping down to the shore. You pass Sakonnet Vineyards, a commercial winery that is open to visitors. After another few miles, you reach the center of Little Compton. The long triangular green is framed by a handsome white church, an old-fashioned country store (in the same building since 1893), and a weathered cemetery where Elizabeth Pabodie, daughter of John and Priscilla Alden and the first Caucasian girl born in New England, is buried.

The route heads north from the village along narrow lanes through a more wooded area. The Pachet Brook Reservoir is on your left; proceed north through forests and small farms back to the starting point.

The 35-mile ride heads toward the ocean in Westport, Massachusetts. Just before the state line, you can visit unspoiled South Shore Beach, a half mile off the route, by turning right instead of left at the end of Shaw Road. Just beyond it, accessible only on foot, is Goosewing Beach, an even lovelier area, owned by the Nature Conservancy. In Westport, bike along the windswept coast, an unspoiled strand framed by salt ponds and cedar-shingled homes. At its eastern tip is the exclusive summer colony of Acoaxet. From here you have a relaxing ride to Adamsville, 100 yards across the Rhode Island line in Little Compton, following the west branch of the Westport River. In the village are a country store in a rambling old wooden building, a monument to the Rhode Island Red breed of poultry, and Stone Bridge Dishes, makers of fine china. A long, step-like climb north of Adamsville rejoins you with the 25-mile ride, where you'll pass through woods and small farms back to the starting point.

The two longer rides can be extended by following Route 77 south of Meeting House Lane all the way to Sakonnet Point, the southernmost spot on the east side of the bay, with its nearly 360-degree panorama of ocean views. It's about 7.5 miles from Meeting House Lane to Sakonnet Point and back.

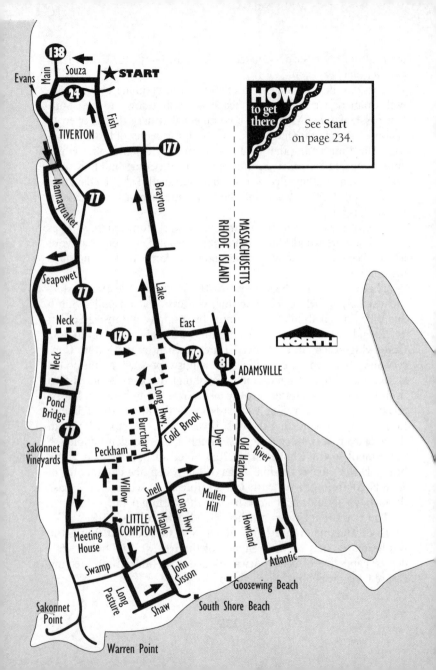

HOW to get there See Start on page 234.

- Head west on Souza Road, opposite the parking lot (don't get on Fish Road). Go 0.8 mile to end (Main Road, unmarked).
- Left for 0.5 mile to Evans Avenue on right, just after going over Route 24.
- Right for 0.9 mile to end (merge right on Route 77). *Caution:* Steep, curving descent to Sakonnet River with sand at bottom. Please take it easy.
- Bear right for 1.2 miles to Nannaquaket Road on right.
- Right across bridge for 1.6 miles to yield sign (merge right onto Route 77).
- Bear right for 0.5 mile to small crossroads (Seapowet Avenue on right).
- Right for 2.2 miles to where Neck Road (unmarked) turns left and the main road bears right. Here the 17-mile ride turns left.
- Bear right for 1.3 miles to first left (Pond Bridge Road), just past top of hill.
- Left for 0.5 mile to end (Route 77).
- Right for 3.6 miles to Meeting House Lane (unmarked) on left, at traffic island (sign may say TO THE COMMONS). Sakonnet Vineyards on left after 1.5 miles.
- Left for 0.6 mile to fork, at Little Compton green.
- Bear right for 0.2 mile to end, in center of Little Compton. Here the 25-mile ride turns left.
- Right for 1.2 miles to end (Swamp Road on right, Brownell Road on left).
- Right and just ahead left on Long Pasture Road (unmarked). Go 0.6 mile to end (Shaw Road, unmarked).
- Left for 0.5 mile to end. Here the ride turns left, but if you turn right for 0.5 mile, you'll come to South Shore Beach, with Goosewing Beach beyond it.
- Left for 0.5 mile to John Sisson Road (unmarked) on right.
- Right for 1.9 miles to fork where one branch bears right and the other branch goes straight. It's immediately after a stop sign.

237

- Bear right for 0.9 mile to another fork where main road curves right at traffic island.
- Curve right for 0.8 mile to end.
- Right for 0.5 mile to Howland Road on right.
- Right for 1.1 miles to Atlantic Avenue on left, just before ocean.
- Left for 0.7 mile to end. Here the ride turns left, but if you turn right, a dirt road leads 0.5 mile to high boulder at tip of peninsula, with a great view.
- Left for 3.3 miles to stop sign (merge right).
- Bear right for 0.5 mile to end, in village of Adamsville.
- Left and just ahead right on Route 81 for 1.5 miles to East Road (unmarked) on left.
- Left for 1.1 miles to crossroads (Lake Road). This is a step-like climb with several short, steep pitches.
- Right for 2.2 miles to Brayton Road on left.
- Left for 1.8 miles to stop sign and blinking light (Route 177, Bulgarmarsh Road).
- Left for 0.8 mile to Fish Road (unmarked) on right.
- Right for 1.5 miles to parking lot on right, just past Route 24.

25 miles

- Follow first 12 directions of long ride, to center of Little Compton.
- Left and just ahead straight on Willow Avenue for 1.4 miles to end (Peckham Road, unmarked).
- Right for 0.3 mile to Burchard Avenue (unmarked) on left, almost at top of hill.
- Left for 1.5 miles to end (Long Highway, unmarked).
- Left for 1.6 miles to crossroads and stop sign (Route 179, East Road).
- Straight for 2.2 miles to Brayton Road (unmarked) on left.
- Follow last 3 directions of 35-mile ride.

17 miles

- Follow first 7 directions of 35-mile ride, to where Neck Road (unmarked) turns left and the main road bears right.

- Left for 0.8 mile to traffic light (Route 77, Main Road). Gray's Ice Cream on far right corner.
- Straight for 1.6 miles to crossroads (Lake Road). This stretch is a gradual climb.
- Left for 2.2 miles to Brayton Road (unmarked) on left.
- Follow last 3 directions of 35-mile ride.

	Historic Sites	Unique Spots	Ocean/Bay Views	Lakes, Ponds, Dams
1 Tri-State Tour				L
2 Putnam–Thompson–Woodstock	L			●
3 Burrillville				●
4 Northern Border Ride				
5 Smithfield–North Smithfield	L			●
6 Lincoln Loop				●
7 Blackstone Valley Tour	●			L
8 Cumberland–Wrentham				●
9 South Attleboro–Cumberland				●
10 Ray Young's Ride				
11 Chepachet–Scituate–Foster		L		●
12 Scituate Spins				●
13 Scituate–Foster		●		●
14 West Cranston–Hope–Scituate				L
15 Providence East Side	●	●	●	
16 Coventry–West Greenwich		●		●
17 East Greenwich–North Kingstown	●	●	●	
18 Connecticut Border				●
19 That Dam Ride		●		●
20 Richmond–Carolina–Shannock		●		
21 Wickford–Kingston	●		●	
22 Bay and Beaches	L	●	●	
23 Wakefield–Narragansett	●	●	●	
24 Jonnycake Ride	●	●		L
25 Kingston–Shannock–Matunuck	L	●	L	
26 South County: Chariho			L	
27 Cows and Casinos		L		
28 Westerly–Watch Hill	●	●	●	
29 Block Island	●	●	●	
30 East Providence–Riverside	●	●	●	

L = Long Ride only

S = Short Ride only

Mill Villages	New England Villages	Open Land, Views	Easy	Hilly	
●	●				1
L	●	●		●	2
●	●				3
●	●	L			4
●	●				5
		●			6
●		●		●	7
		L			8
	S	●			9
L		●			10
	L			●	11
	●				12
	S			●	13
●					14
					15
	●			●	16
					17
●	●	●		●	18
L	L				19
L	L	L			20
	●	L	S		21
●					22
			S		23
L	●		S		24
L	●				25
●	●				26
	●	●			27
L	●		S		28
		●			29
			●		30

241

	Historic Sites	Unique Spots	Ocean/Bay Views	Lakes, Ponds, Dams
31 Seekonk–Attleboro–Norton		●		L
32 Seekonk–Rehoboth North				●
33 Seekonk–Rehoboth South				●
34 Seekonk–Rehoboth: *One More Time*				L
35 Swansea–Somerset–Dighton	L		L	S
36 Barrington Ride			●	●
37 Along the Bay	●	●	●	
38 Jamestown Ride	●	●	●	
39 Middletown–Portsmouth	●		●	●
40 Newport–Middletown	●	●	●	
41 Tiverton–Little Compton		L	●	

Mill Villages	New England Villages	Open Land, Views	Easy	Hilly	
	L		●		**31**
	L				**32**
	●	●	●		**33**
	●				**34**
	●		S		**35**
			●		**36**
					37
	●				**38**
		●	●		**39**
			S		**40**
	L	●	S		**41**

Appendix

Bicycle shops

Shops are listed alphabetically by town. Area code is 401 unless otherwise specified.

Union Cycle, 77 Pleasant Street, Attleboro, MA. (508) 226–4726

Block Island Bike Rental, Ocean Avenue, Block Island. 466–2297
Old Harbor Bike Shop, Old Harbor, Block Island (rentals only). 466–2029

Coventry Mountain Bikes, 982 Tiogue Avenue, Coventry. 826–8030
Greenway Cycles, 579 Washington Street, Coventry. 822–2080

Bicycle Joe's Bike Shop, 1985 Broad Street, Cranston. 941–0006
Bicycle Works, 155 Park Avenue, Cranston. 941–2268

The Cycle Works, 1000 Mendon Road, Cumberland. 333–2520

Al's Ordinary Bike Shop, 21 Furnace Street, Danielson, CT.
(860) 774–1660

East Providence Cycle, 414 Warren Avenue, East Providence. 434–3838

Crosby Cycle Company, 398 Rhode Island Avenue, Fall River, MA. (508)
679–9366

B&B Cycle, 149 Reservoir Avenue, Lincoln. 725–2830

Island Sports, 86 Aquidneck Avenue, Middletown. 846–4421
Pedal Power Bicycle Shop, 879 West Main Road, Middletown. 846–7525

Narragansett Bikes, 1153 Boston Neck Road, Narragansett. 782–4444

Adventure Sports, Inn at Long Wharf, Newport (rentals only). 849–4820
Newport Bicycle, 162 Broadway, Newport. 846–0773
Newport Wheelsports, 561 Thames Street, Newport (rentals only).
849–4400
Ten Speed Spokes, 18 Elm Street, Newport. 847–5609

Epicycle, 345 East Washington Street, North Attleboro, MA. (508)
643–2453

Sirois Bicycle Shop, 893 Landry Avenue, North Attleboro, MA. (508) 695–6303

Ron's Bicycle Shop, 7592 Post Road, North Kingstown. 294–2238

Mottola Bicycle, 24 Sayles Avenue, Pascoag. 568–2228

Downing Bicycles, 795 Hope Street, Providence. 831–2453
Esta's Too, 257 Thayer Street, Providence. 831–2651
Providence Bicycle, 725 Branch Avenue, Providence. 331–6610
Rainbow Bicycles, 144 Brook Street, Providence. 861–6176

Silver Bicycles, 6 Livery Street, Putnam, CT. (860) 928–7370

East Providence Cycle, 111 Crescent View Avenue, Riverside. 437–2453
Your Bike Shop, 459 Willett Avenue, Riverside. 433–4491

National Ski & Bike, 102 Washington Street, South Attleboro, MA. (508) 761–4500

Bike Line of Swansea, 79 Swansea Mall Drive, Swansea, MA. (508) 677–0710

W. E. Stedman Company, 196 Main Street, Wakefield. 789–8664

Your Bike Shop, 51 Cole Street, Warren. 245–9755

Bald Hill Mountain Bikes, 1000 Bald Hill Road, Warwick. 821–0670
Caster's Bicycle Center, 3480 Post Road, Warwick. 739–0393
Rounds of Cycling, 1415 Warwick Avenue, Warwick. 463–3570
Ski Market, 500 Greenwich Avenue, Warwick. 732–6390

King's Cyclery, 271 Post Road, Westerly. 322–6005
Ray Willis Bicycles, 53 Railroad Avenue, Westerly. 596–1045

A. A. Vittorio Cycle, 583 Wood Avenue, Woonsocket. 765–3275
Darling Cycle, 215 Arnold Street, Woonsocket. 769–6388
Izzy's Sports, 403 Park Avenue, Woonsocket. 762–9550

Al's Bicycles, 1171 Main Street, Wyoming. 539–7540